UNTANGLING THE LAW:

Strategies for Legal Writers

UNTANGLING THE LAW:
Strategies for Legal Writers

Kristin R. Woolever

NORTHEASTERN UNIVERSITY

Wadsworth Publishing Company
Belmont, California
A Division of Wadsworth, Inc.

English Editor: John Strohmeier
Special Projects Editor: Lorraine Anderson
Editorial Assistant: Holly Allen
Production Editor: Jerilyn Emori
Managing Designer: Merle Sanderson
Print Buyer: Ruth Cole
Designer: Detta Penna
Copy Editor: Sylvia Stein
Technical Illustrator: Susan Breitbard
Cover: Ingbritt Christensen

Printed in the United States of America   **49**

1 2 3 4 5 6 7 8 9 10—91 90 89 88 87

Library of Congress Cataloging-in-Publication Data
Woolever, Kristin R.
  Untangling the law: strategies for legal writers.
  Includes index.
  1. Legal composition.   I. Title.
KF250.W66 1987   808′.06634   86-24679
ISBN 0-534-07488-X

Contents

Preface

The average lawyer writes more than the average novelist.
WILLIAM PROSSER*

Untangling the Law: Strategies for Legal Writers is a book for practicing attorneys, law students, paralegals—anyone in the legal profession who writes. Its main premise is that lawyers need to know as much about the craft of writing as they do about the legal profession because the law's lifeblood is its language.

In their daily routines, attorneys write client letters, memoranda, briefs, and a variety of other documents for various audiences and purposes. Yet most of their training has ignored writing as an important aspect of the profession. This book's seven chapters fill the gap by focusing solely on the legal writing process, not on research methods or on legal issues. It is designed for attorneys to use as a reference when they want to fine-tune their writing techniques or for law students to use as a supplement to their substantive law books. In its organization and in its problem-solving approach to writing, *Untangling the Law* provides specific advice for attorneys who want to write forcefully in a variety of problematic situations.

*William Prosser, "English as She Is Wrote," in *Advocacy and the King's English*, George Rossman, ed. (Indianapolis: Bobbs-Merrill, 1960).

THE POLITICS OF THE WRITING SITUATION

A feature that makes this book different is its attention to reader psychology as a primary consideration for attorneys designing legal documents. To communicate effectively, lawyers need to be clear and concise but also to have a sense of the politics involved in each writing task. From the first chapter on audience analysis to the discussions of paragraphing and sentence-level editing, this book focuses on the reader's response to the attorney's prose. Some writing situations require more formal language than others; some require subtle innuendo rather than direct confrontational prose; some demand carefully objective explanations. The more the writers understand about readers' perspectives, the more control they have over the writing process.

Beginning where good writers should begin, with audience analysis, *Untangling the Law* moves through the drafting process, concentrating on organizational strategies and specific editing techniques—all based on a thorough understanding of situational psychology.

HOW THIS BOOK IS ORGANIZED

The book is organized from the top down. It starts with preliminary planning, moves to organization of the whole document, then to the smaller scale organization of the paragraph, before getting down to editing sentences. As a step-by-step guide through the writing process, such organization makes sense because it follows the same process writers follow when they compose. The final two chapters of the book, Chapters 6 and 7, apply the previous chapters' suggestions to specific purposes. Chapter 6 focuses on writing as an advocate, putting writing techniques to use in persuasive situations. Chapter 7 illustrates how legal writing changes when the writer moves from analysis to advocacy; the chapter compares an office memorandum and a trial brief on the same case.

Unlike many legal writing textbooks, *Untangling the Law* is not organized as a writing handbook containing grammar rules and traditional formulas for standard legal prose. Instead, it contains practical advice for professional-level writers who need to upgrade their techniques for written argument, analysis, and explanations of law. The emphasis is on style and organizational strategies, not on mechanics or grammar. When necessary, the chapters provide "Quick Review" sections to refresh the memory on basic grammar and sentence structure needed to write powerful prose. Short and to the point, these sections serve as reference more than as detailed explanation.

The book is short and easy to use. It complements any legal research manual or other text explaining the major types and functions of legal documents. It's equally useful as an attorney's quick reference or as a law student's textbook, and its basic premise is not one that will go out of date: Clear professional writing is a craft worthy of significant attention. This book operates on that principle.

USE OF CASE FILES

A special feature of the book is its use of case files. All of the many examples threaded throughout the text are taken from the two cases that form the Appendix. Users of the text, if they take a few minutes to read these cases first, will feel at home with all of the examples used to illustrate specific points and techniques. They therefore won't have to puzzle through new fact patterns and new legal issues with every example given.

But there is another reason for turning to the Appendix and reading the case files before beginning the text. To emphasize the problem-solving approach the book takes, each chapter begins with a problem—an example of problematic prose written about the two cases. The subsequent pages then discuss techniques for correcting the problem, and the actual problem solution appears at the end of the chapter. If readers think about the problems before reading on, they will find the chapters more meaningful because the discussion will parallel their own thinking.

ACKNOWLEDGMENTS

Without the help of these people, *Untangling the Law* would have remained a tangle of ideas. My sincere thanks to Brook K. Baker, assistant professor of law at Northeastern University, for reading endless drafts of the manuscript and serving as both mentor and guinea pig; to James V. Rowan, professor of law at Northeastern, for having enough confidence in me to suggest I write the book and for much encouragement along the way; to John Strohmeier, English editor at Wadsworth, and all the other fine people there who worked with me on this project; to Chris Rideout, director of the Legal Writing Institute and assistant professor of English and legal writing at the University of Puget Sound, for his editing expertise and his continued professional advice; to Barbara Cox, University of Wisconsin; Michele Minnis, University of New Mexico; Laurel Oates, University of Puget Sound; Diana Pratt, Wayne State University; Michael Stamp, Monterey College of Law; Sandra Verhoogen, Hastings College; and Richard Wydick, University of California at Davis, who reviewed the manuscript and helped shape the book; and special thanks to Chris Shipley for editing, typing, and enduring.

More than any others, the students at Northeastern University Law School (1983–1986) deserve credit and thanks.

Chapter 1

Introduction: Approaching Legal Writing

Most books about legal writing focus more on "legal" than on "writing." This one is different. Its subject isn't legal research or legal method. Instead, it explains how to write clearly and forcefully in the legal profession.

At the heart of this text is the assumption that legal writing is the art of using language to make something happen. Each writing task requires different skills to achieve the desired results. Lawyers whose prose is a tangle of research and legal formulae confuse rather than clarify the issues. They've put so much energy into research that they've neglected the means to express their findings. Instead of using language to control the situation, lawyers often lose authority when they sit down to write.

THE LAW AS A SEAMLESS WEB

"The law is a seamless web," law professors are fond of reminding their students. The lightest touch on any strand sends vibrations through the entire intricate structure. Every legal issue, rule, and theory is connected; thus attention to any part affects the whole. Ironically, the metaphor's appropriateness extends beyond this initial image because the slightest vibrations running through even the most beautiful web alert the waiting spider— the beauty disguises a deadly trap.

Primary victims are law students and new associates, who often become obsessed with the intricate system of legal relationships. Intent on making connections, on leaving nothing untouched, they may ensnare themselves in webs of words and become unable to regain the freedom of clarity. This compulsion to discuss simultaneously all threads of these interwoven legal relationships afflicts every level of composing, from organizing the overall document to structuring each paragraph and designing each sentence. It also trips up writers at nearly every level of the legal profession, from law students to veteran lawyers—even judges.

STATUTORY LANGUAGE VERSUS PLAIN LANGUAGE

Adding to the confusion for both writer and reader are the two distinct languages of the law: statutory language and plain language. In the legal profession, both languages are necessary, but each has a specific purpose. Problems arise when attorneys aren't aware of the differences between the two and use inflated statutory language as their primary form of communication.

"Statutory language" (the language of statutes and other legal rules) is constructed to stand the test of time. The precise phrasing of legal contracts, wills, and treaties serves the same purpose and also falls under this rubric. The wording must be applicable the day it is drafted as well as years into the future, when lawyers will rely on it to measure situations as yet undetermined. That's why statutory language contains so many qualifiers and apparently redundant descriptive clauses in an attempt to be precise. Such style sacrifices grace and clarity for the precision necessary to last for generations and to serve as the arbiter of future disputes. For example, this paragraph comes from a standard apartment lease:

> **Statutory language:**
> If the leased premises, or any part thereof, or the whole or any part thereof of the building of which they are a part, shall be taken for any purpose by exercise of the power of eminent domain or condemnation, or by action of the city or other authorities or shall receive any direct or consequential damage for which the Lessor or Lessee shall be entitled to compensation by reason of anything lawfully done in pursuance of any public authority after the execution hereof and during said term, or any extension or renewal thereof, then at the option of either the Lessor or Lessee, this lease and said term shall terminate and such option may be exercised in the case of any such taking, notwithstanding the entire interest of the Lessor or Lessee may have been divested by such taking. (From the Boston Rental Housing Authority's standard form apartment lease, subsection 9)

Plain language is not meant to stand as law, but to communicate efficiently and directly. Legal briefs, memoranda, and other forms of legal writing should speak to the present, not remain classic statements for years to come. For instance, the plain version of the apartment lease makes its point quickly and understandably for the average person:

Plain language:
If city authorities take over the leased premises or cause some damage to the premises, then the Lessor or the Lessee has the option to end the lease.

Even case law falls into this category because appellate judges' rulings apply the law to specific, timely situations. Clear, expository writing expressing appellate court decisions is more valuable to attorneys who refer to these cases than prose burdened by legal qualifiers—attempting to stand as absolute precedent for all similar circumstances. *Stare decisis* is flexible, not static, in actual practice, and the most useful higher court interpretations of the law are those clearly and forcefully stated.

When lawyers write a trial brief or an office memorandum, they must include the key statutory language that applies to the case, but they need to see the difference between that formal prose and the common language surrounding it. Too often the distinction between the two is vague as writers eager to impress—or writers simply confused—turn an everyday communication task into the Bill of Rights. Here's an example from an office memorandum, a document addressed to the writer's colleagues:

Based on the elusive distinction between different kinds of injuries and in response to conflicting policies between the worker's compensation system, statutes prohibiting discriminatory employment practices, and traditional common law actions for breaches of contract and dignatory torts, the Michigan Court of Appeals has evolved, through a series of instructive decisions, an unfinished rule which bifurcates the remedies available to a wrongfully discharged employee, namely that his or her disability is solely compensable before the Worker's Compensation Bureau, that his or her contract damages are redressable in civil litigation and that his or her other damages, including emotional distress and loss of professional esteem may or may not be compensable in tort depending on how analogous the claim is to one under discrimination statutes.

There surely are simpler ways to decide if the client can take civil action against the employer who wrongfully fired her. Even after reading this paragraph several times, most experienced attorneys would have difficulty understanding the main point. But the writer argues proudly that she is now "writing like a lawyer," though she is not connecting with *any* audience, legal or otherwise.

Although this is an exaggeration, it exemplifies a problem common to nearly all lawyers who write. Because attorneys are so used to reading the statutory language of the law itself, they often mimic its serpentine style every time they sit down to write. This practice has spread to such an extent that, in many instances, law students who arrive at school able to write perfectly clear prose deliberately adopt this ornate, unreadable style. New associates in law firms often do the same thing in an attempt to sound impressive. This misconception of sonorous legal writing as a means of impressing the audience is certainly more writer directed than aimed for the reader. It also indicates the writer's confusion about the function of legal language.

HOW TO USE THIS BOOK

This book offers specific advice on how to untangle convoluted prose and get on with the business of communicating clearly. Before reading any of the other chapters, turn first to the Appendix, where you'll find two case files: *Vivian Casterbank* v. *The South End Family Planning Clinic* and *William Revere* v. *Jan Wharton, et al.* Familiarize yourself with the case facts and the characters because these legal problems provide all the examples in the book. The first case involves Vivian Casterbank, a nurse fired after refusing to assist with an abortion. She is suing the South End Clinic for breach of contract. The second case involves William Revere, a guest at a party who fell into a ten-foot hole in a darkened renovation area. He is taking action against property owner Jan Wharton for negligence in not adequately safeguarding the danger.

Lawyers are problem solvers, and these cases provide the writing problems the following chapters show you how to solve. Beginning with audience analysis, the text follows the attorney step by step through the drafting process, giving the rationale for each step. Chapters 2–6 begin with a problem the writer must solve before moving on to the next step in the writing process. For instance, a lawyer who hasn't clearly defined the audience can't make legitimate organizational decisions. A writer who hasn't determined the overall organization can't forcefully compose individual sentences.

Controlling language so that the relationship of the words creates a dynamic, persuasive effect is a skill lawyers hold in especially high regard. William Prosser suggests, "Lawyers must use that double-edged tool, the English language, with all the precision of a surgeon handling a scalpel."* The required precision intimidates many writers.

To write well, you need a clear strategy for the whole drafting process—from outline to finished document. *Untangling the Law* provides commonsense writing tips and strategies to help unravel the mysteries of legal writing for the writer and subsequently for the reader. That's what this book is about: a nononsense approach to legal writing.

---

*William Prosser, "English as She Is Wrote," in *Advocacy and the King's English*, George Rossman, ed. (Indianapolis: Bobbs-Merrill, 1960).

Chapter 2

Analyzing Audience, Purpose, Tone

Problem

Read the following problem statements concerning the *Revere* v. *Wharton* case. Although they deal with similar legal questions, they differ in many important ways. Take a few minutes before reading Chapter 2 and consider the differences between Problem A and Problem B. It might help to make a list of these differences and to pay particular attention to the tone of each problem. Who is the intended audience, and what is the purpose of each?

Problem A:

1.   Under the 1974 Tenement Building and Multiple Premises Act, is Wharton, the landlord of One Traverso Street, liable to Revere, a tenant's social guest, for personal injuries resulting from Wharton's failure to inspect, safeguard, or issue warnings concerning the open door, the renovations, and the dangerous hole in or accessible from first floor common areas?

2.   Is the Court likely to decide issues of common area liability as a matter of law at summary judgment or are there disputed facts or law/fact issues making summary judgment inappropriate?

Problem B:

1.   Could a jury conclude that the defendant landlord gave William Revere reason to believe that the open doorway leading off of the first floor common foyer led to common areas available for his use as a prospective tenant and a tenant's lawful guest?

2.   May defendant landlord be liable to William Revere for negligently permitting his foreseeable access from the first floor common foyer to the dangerous renovation area immediately beyond the open door?

3.   Could a jury conclude that defendant landlord breached her duty to inspect the common foyer and the accessible renovation area during her three-hour attendance at a tenant's party or that she breached her duty to issue proper warnings to unsuspecting guests concerning the known ongoing dangerous renovations?

4.   Could a jury conclude that defendant landlord had sufficient notice of the dangerous hole and sufficient op-

portunity to observe the open door to be charged with actual knowledge of these dangerous conditions?

The problem solution appears at the end of the chapter.

Although practicing attorneys have been paying increasing attention to the elements of good legal writing, their emphasis is often in the wrong place. Most faculty who teach law students to write focus on *revision* as the key to effective legal drafting. Although lawyers thoroughly prepare in advance for other aspects of their practice, they often view writing as the one area that affords the luxury of hasty preparation followed by edit upon edit. The bulk of their preliminary work consists of extensive legal research at the expense of paying attention to the psychology of the rhetorical situation.

The entire process of legal writing can be shorter and more effective if the writer emphasizes the beginning rather than the end of the drafting situation. To do that requires two considerations: (1) understanding audience, purpose, and tone, the three dramatic elements in the rhetorical situation and (2) recognizing how those elements apply to the four major types of legal writing. This chapter discusses both of these preliminary considerations and suggests that such preparation is as essential to the writing process as similar preparation is to the oral advocacy process.

DEFINING THE RHETORICAL SITUATION

The first step to clear writing is a clear understanding of the document's audience and its purpose. This presents a special problem for lawyers because they must not only define the complex legal issues of a case, but also analyze the relationship between purpose and audience in order to determine the most effective tone.

Three elements—audience, purpose, and tone—compose the rhetorical situation. Writing for one audience is complicated, but lawyers have the added burden of interpreting the law for multiple audiences during the course of each case. Many legal writers are so caught up in analyzing the issues that they overlook the concept of an audience for their written work. They then write without considering these readers' needs.

Communicating effectively means transferring information from one person to another. Legal writers must recognize the relationship among the dramatic elements in written documents as clearly as they recognize the drama in oral advocacy. Attorneys have little problem understanding this interplay in oral argument because the audience is in front of them, reacting to the rhetoric. But the oral advocacy stage—bringing to mind the drama of Perry Mason or Clarence Darrow—is the "glory end" of litigation. Few cases even make it to jury trial. Even in those that do, the bulk of the convincing comes in the letters, memos, and briefs written before the attorneys' final appeals to the jury. Each of these documents is a rhetorical instrument in which the reader's nature plays a large role in how the writer organizes the material and chooses language to elicit the desired response. The legal writer's audience—judges, lawyers, and clients—will resist a self-directed monologue, just as members of a jury would be non-plussed if an advocate didn't talk directly to them. Every dynamic trial lawyer learns this lesson early: the more you connect with your audience, the more control you have over the situation. The same holds true for writing. In either writing or speaking, connecting with the audience means understanding its needs.

To understand your audience's needs in legal writing, begin by directing your attention to your readers. First you need to consider the common legal audiences, then the most common purposes for legal writing, and finally, how audience and purpose determine tone. If you take the time to understand these elements of the rhetorical situation before you write, the actual writing process is much easier.

Quick Review

Rhetorical situation means that someone is trying to communicate information or an opinion to another person or group of people. Such an inherently dramatic situation occurs whether the communication is oral or written. Similar to stage drama or the drama of a good novel, the rhetorical

> situation in legal writing contains the three dramatic elements of audience, purpose, and tone. The interplay of these elements determines the success or failure of the communicating process.

FOUR COMMON LEGAL AUDIENCES

The first thing legal writers need to consider is exactly who is the audience for each document. Lawyers generally write for four specific audiences:

- clients
- law office partners and associates
- opposing attorneys
- judges and the courts

Each of these audiences requires a different approach to effectively communicate with them. The following ten questions should help you become more aware of your audience and better able to find the right approach. Taking the time to answer these questions before you begin writing will familiarize you with your multidimensional audience. It's always easier to make connections with people you know than with people who aren't familiar to you. As you read, notice that the questions force you to pin down specifics about your readers while also placing them in a context (a busy law office, a hostile courtroom, a political situation, etc.). By knowing these specifics in advance, you can tailor your prose to meet the audience's needs.

1. Who is the primary audience?

2. If there is more than one audience for the document, will you need to concentrate on one at the expense of the other?

3. What is the audience's education level?

4. What knowledge of the law does the audience have?

5. If the audience is an attorney, what legal specialty does he or she have?

6.   What history does this audience have with similar legal matters?

7.   Are there biases or prejudices present?

8.   How many years of experience does the audience have on the job?

9.   Under what circumstances will the audience read the document?

10.   Are there any external pressures that might influence how the audience will interpret the document?

Once you've answered these questions and have a fairly detailed portrait of your particular audience, the next step is to place this specific reader against the background of other common legal audiences. Seeing the specific against the general field allows you to understand some of the common reader needs you haven't previously discovered. And it also serves to sharpen the contrast between your audience and the others in the general category. By cross-checking the ten questions with the four common legal audiences, you can see precisely how your reader fits in.

Clients

What does the client need from your writing? First, he or she needs to understand how you are proceeding with the case and why you've chosen certain methods. Second, the client needs to feel secure in your handling of the case. Third, the client does *not* want to be patronized.

Before you write a client letter or any interrogatory material to which the client must respond, consider questions 3, 4, and 6. (What is the client's education level, legal knowledge, and history with similar legal matters?) Generally, clients are afraid of the litigation process when they have a limited understanding of legal language. When you understand how the client is likely to respond to certain rhetoric, you can tailor your words to fit that audience and offer appropriate reassurance.

It's especially hard for most attorneys to step outside of esoteric legal language and explain complex matters of law to lay people. The following examples illustrate attempts to explain to a client the Court's probable view of Jan Wharton and Nelson

Rayman's working relationship. The writers hold different opinions about the relationship, and they certainly express these opinions in widely varied fashions:

Example 1:
It is not dispositive of the employee/employer relationship if the Renovation Agreement uses the terms "contractee"/"contractor." The majority of Texas precedents that support Rayman's employee status under the Renovation Agreement stem from Worker's Compensation cases. Granted, in these cases the Courts employ a liberal construction of the employee definition as a matter of public policy; but, in the absence of statutory authority, the determination of employee within the meaning of the act is to be determined by the application of common law torts.

Example 2:
Wharton, as owner of the building at One Traverso Street, will be held vicariously liable for the negligence of Nelson Rayman. In order to prove this, we will have to show that Rayman is Wharton's employee. Rayman's status as an employee will be established by the amount of control Wharton has over the details of the job. Texas tests the amount of control by looking at a number of elements that, taken together, indicate what the relationship is. The more control Wharton has, the more likely it is that Rayman is an employee. Conversely, the more control Rayman has, the more likely it is that he is an independent contractor.

Most attorneys would have difficulty reading the first example with its proliferation of legal terms and its lack of focus. And a lay reader would certainly be at a loss to understand "public policy," "statutory authority," and "common law torts." The second example, however, uses language any intelligent person can understand, and the explanation proceeds in a focused, step-by-step fashion. Such prose speaks directly to the client without sounding patronizing or pompous.

Law Office Partners and Associates

Your associates are busy people who need information they can read quickly and trust explicitly. It's nice to know this audience is usually not hostile or looking for ways to undermine what you say. The key to writing for this audience is to determine what they already know so you can organize the material to best suit their needs, leaving out extraneous facts and other information. Of special importance to the writer here are questions 5, 6, and 8—all of which explore the familiarity these lawyers might have with relevant legal issues (legal specialty, history with similar cases, experience on the job). Question 9 (Under what circumstances will the audience read the document?) is important to consider as well. Your associates want a document that comes to the point quickly, lists the possible alternatives, and "reads" efficiently. That means you shouldn't waste time with lengthy explanations or unnecessary facts, and you should organize the analysis deductively under clear headings.

For example, knowing the audience's needs would have helped the writer leave out some of the irrelevant information in this fact description:

> On 20 July 1983, William Revere attended a party in Paul Cohen's apartment. The apartment building, located at One Traverso Street, was owned by Jan Wharton, also a party guest that evening. The building was undergoing renovation at the time, and some of the apartments were incomplete. Prior to the renovations, the building had been an old warehouse that Wharton purchased at a tax sale in January 1973. In addition to residential apartments, Wharton intended to rent some space on the first floor to commercial businesses.

An attorney who wants to know only the necessary facts doesn't need to know about the tax sale or about Wharton's plans to use the first floor for commercial rents. Even more problematic is the writer's lack of deductive order for any of the information presented, giving the reader no connections between the facts and no framework in which to understand them. In this paragraph, the facts are presented out of a meaningful context. (Chapter 3 gives specific tips for polishing these deductive organizing techniques.)

Opposing Attorneys

In most instances, the opposing attorneys are the secondary audience of documents designed for the Court or for the client. The counsel for the defendant may receive copies of documents written by the plaintiff's attorneys and vice versa, even though the primary reader is a judge or the clients themselves (as in interrogatories). But the opposition is an especially difficult audience. Nothing would please the opponent more than for you to sacrifice your own point of view by spending the majority of your document in rebuttal. Although you must keep the opponent in mind as you write, resist the temptation to write *for* him or her. Instead, try to find common ground between the primary and secondary audiences (question 2) and proceed from there. If that's not possible, the best defense in this rhetorical jousting match is a good offense. Anticipate the opponent's plan of attack and probable reaction to your argument by applying question 7 (Are there biases or prejudices present?) and questions 6 and 8 (history with similar cases, experience on the job). Then deal with the opposing view *within* your own argument. Never feature the opponent's view first.

Remember that the writer can best quiet the opposition by remaining calm while stealing the opponent's thunder. The more of the opposing argument you can anticipate and defend against, the less effective the opponent will be. For example, the following argument anticipates a counterattack and handles it nicely. In the italicized final sentence, notice how calmly William Revere's attorney parries what might have been a damaging point, but she deflects the blow while remaining the aggressor:

> Wharton may attempt to obtain summary judgment on four common area issues: (1) that the renovation area was not common; (2) that she had no knowledge of the open door or dangerous hole; (3) that she may not be held liable for negligently permitting access to the noncommon renovation area; and (4) that she breached no duty of care, even of inspection, with respect to the common area. *Although there is some support for deciding premises liability issues as a matter of law on undisputed facts, there are reasonable inferences and jury questions on the boundaries of the common areas, Wharton's knowledge of the dangers, and her breach of her duty of care.*

Judges and the Courts

For most legal writers, judges and the courts are the ultimate—and most intimidating—audience. In this dramatic situation, the speaker/writer must use rhetorical prowess to convince the audience of a particular viewpoint. Often entire cases are decided upon the basis of the documents the attorneys prepare for the court, so it's no wonder many writers spend hours and hours honing their arguments. Language is a powerful persuasive tool when wielded skillfully. Memoranda to the court, trial briefs, appellate briefs, and so forth require special attention to the nature of the audience. In addition to the obviously applicable questions (6 and 7 again), two others come to the forefront in this rhetorical situation—questions 8 and 10:

- *How experienced is the judge?*
  Novice judges may respond more readily to psychologically "loaded" language than veteran judges, who are more used to hearing such slanted arguments.

- *Are there any external pressures that may influence the judge's interpretation of the document?*
  These pressures can include anything from the judge's political aspirations to public policy issues. Try to determine the judge's special interests and appeal to them if possible.

Exemplifying how a writer can reap the benefits of external pressures on the audience, the following memorandum to the court clearly calls upon the judge to follow in the footsteps of the "classic" precedents. In this instance, the lawyer has gambled on the judge's sensitivity to such issues:

> Summary judgment on Count II should be denied both because several law-fact issues in this case have historically been left for the jury and because certain material facts are in substantial dispute. For example, juries have consistently determined the exact boundaries of disputed common areas. Likewise, whether defendant breached her legal duties is also a classic jury issue. The principal factual dispute concerns Wharton's knowledge about the open door and dangerous hole.

Because the attorney who wrote this memo had a definite concept of his audience (the novice judge), he has exerted just enough pressure to make it difficult for the judge to break with tradition and grant summary judgment in this case. The key here is the writer's subtle aiming of the language directly at the spot where the reader may be vulnerable.

WRITER-DIRECTED VERSUS READER-DIRECTED PROSE

Doing preliminary research on the intended audience allows you to know your reader well enough to develop effective strategies. But if you're like most writers, even after extensive audience analysis, you compose a document's first draft more for yourself than for the reader. Until you have your own ideas clear, it's hard to concentrate on clarifying them for someone else. It's often not until the second draft that writers apply the audience information they've collected and write more for the readers than for themselves. Rhetoricians call this revising process a transformation from "writer-directed prose" to "reader-directed prose." The process sounds easy but is actually extremely difficult.

The first time through a draft, you have probably clarified your order, your thoughts, and your legal research. This version is a weeding-out process, gradually revealing the shape of the argument. If you type this draft and distribute it to the reader, total confusion will probably result unless you can stand by the reader's side deciphering any unclear prose. After countless "What I meant to say here . . ." explanations, you will probably give up, snatch the document, and revise it to answer all the reader's questions.

Perhaps the hardest thing for a writer to realize is that the prose must ultimately stand on its own. The audience will not have the benefit of the writer as coach. To prepare the document for that ultimate separation from the writer, consider again the two things the earlier discussion of audience analysis asked you to think about:

- What does the audience need from this document?

- Does the document directly meet those needs?

If legal writers would occasionally disentangle themselves from their prose and ask these two simple questions, the bulk of legal jargon might disappear. In the fever of composing, writers unwittingly get tangled in explanations and oblique references that create a maze for the reader. Such indirection has no place in legal writing except as evidence that the argument is weak. Sort through the tangle of research cases, opinions, and opposing views, and line them up in clear, linear progression for the reader. Then aim directly for the audience's needs. Remember, the document must represent you without your intervention.

In the following examples, note how the attorney revises the confusing writer-directed prose in the first draft to a second version that's more linear in its order and provides a clear context for the audience:

Writer-directed:

"Right of control" over the mode and method of how the details of work are executed is determinative in the Texas distinction between an "independent contractor" and a "servant." The Texas courts rely most heavily upon the written contract in determining legal status. The Wharton-Rayman contract strongly implies that Rayman was an independent contractor.

Reader-directed:

Our client, Jan Wharton, is being sued by William Revere for personal injuries caused by Nelson Rayman's alleged negligence in renovation of Wharton's warehouse. It is a rule of law in Texas that employers are not vicariously liable for the negligence of their independent contractors, but only for the negligence of their employees. If the Court rules as a matter of law that Rayman's legal status was independent contractor, Wharton cannot be held vicariously liable for Rayman's negligence leading to Revere's injury.

Right of control over work details defines legal status. When determining right of control, the Texas courts rely heavily upon expressed and contractual relations. The Wharton-Rayman contract strongly implies that Rayman's legal status was an independent contractor.

In the second example, the attorney first places the facts in a legal context to immediately orient the audience. From the initial sentence, the reader knows who is suing whom and why. Next, she clearly states the Texas law before explaining how it applies to the Wharton-Rayman contract. Finally, she suggests how the courts probably will view the problem. The writer has targeted the reader, organizing the discussion to increase the readability of the prose. Most readers can understand the whole problem in one quick sitting, without having to reorganize the facts or search for the legal context.

Although concentrating on the reader is essential, this preliminary step is not enough to assure effective communication. By first turning your attention to the audience, you establish a basis for developing a rhetorical plan. The next task is to examine the purpose of the written document in the light of what you have discovered about the audience.

FOUR PURPOSES OF LEGAL WRITING

Lawyers generally concentrate on four kinds of writing: investigative questioning, objective reporting, analyzing, and persuading. To help determine a document's purpose, ask yourself, "What do I want the reader to know or do after reading this document?" The answer to that question is the real purpose of your writing. It's helpful to see the four kinds of legal writing as a continuum, each category a definite part of the process, but each a prerequisite for the next step.

Legal writing category	Purpose
Investigative questioning	To gather information
Objective reporting	To report factual information
Analyzing	To determine how the law applies to the facts
Persuading	To convince an audience that one position is more logical than any other

As with the common legal audiences, these four categories are the general background against which you should place specific writing tasks. Understanding the general context helps writers define their own particular document's purpose.

Investigative Questioning

Lawyers begin every case by gathering information. Client interviews, depositions, and interrogatories are just a few of the writing tasks necessary to the discovery process. For example, in the early discovery stages, attorneys write questions they hope will elicit as much useful information as possible. Most lawyers arrive at deposition hearings with a predrafted outline of possible questions. The outline must be flexible, allowing for whatever twists and turns a live interview will undoubtedly take. When you prepare these questions, you should consider phrasing that best encourages complete answers and that leads naturally to the next question. But first, determine the general purpose:

Q: What do I want the reader to *do* after reading this document?

A: The reader should give me as much factual information as possible and should indicate his or her attitude toward that information.

Depositions

Audience:

The primary audience is deponents, people who may vary widely in expertise and character. If, for instance, the deponent is a medical doctor called for expert testimony, you need to write questions that will establish the doctor's credibility. If the deponent is a nonexpert witness, the questions should elicit factual information—Who? What? When? Where? How? In both instances, the phrasing of the questions should be clearly understandable to the deponent so he or she can answer knowledgeably.

In formal discovery, there is a secondary audience as well: the opponent. The opposing attorney is present at any deposition. Although your primary audience remains the deponent, keep in mind that the opposition can use both the nature of your questions and the resulting answers in preparing the case against you.

The ultimate audience for a deposition may well be a judge or jury called upon to decide facts based on the questions asked and the answers given. Depositions are also used to discredit trial testimony with earlier sworn inconsistencies.

Purpose:

What do depositions help you to do? Primarily, lawyers take depositions to obtain information from witnesses or the opposing party. Secondary purposes can be to confront the deponent with

damaging facts to test his or her story or to evaluate the deponent's behavior under questioning to determine suitability as a
trial witness.

The following excerpt from defendant Jan Wharton's deposition illustrates how the plaintiff's lawyer questions her to obtain as much information as possible to support his client's case.
Note especially the movement toward increasingly specific questions as Attorney Baker tries to establish Wharton's control over
the renovation project.

Q: When you visited the premises, did you have any occasion
    to fire an employee at the job site?

A: Well, I certainly had a lot to do with one guy being let go. I
    don't know whether you'd say I fired him or not, but I went
    down to the site one day and found a fellow smoking dope
    in the basement, and I told him to get off the premises, and
    I told Nelson that this guy ought to pick up his check, and I
    didn't want to see him around again. So you can call it what
    you want, but it was too important a project for me to have
    that kind of thing going on.

Q: And the worker did leave?

A: Oh yeah.

Q: That day?

A: Oh yeah.

Q: Right after you told him he should leave?

A: Right. He left right away.

Even this short excerpt from the questioning illustrates several important techniques. Most important, the attorney has discovered that Wharton will be a good trial witness because she
isn't careful in her answers. Notice that Attorney Baker specifically uses the word "fire" in his question (implying her total
control over the project), and she answers in detail. Second, to
pin down the negative fact and further indicate Wharton's control, Baker asks, "And the worker did leave? . . . That day? . . .
Right after you told him he should leave?" Baker's skillful line of
questioning has served the plaintiff well.

Interrogatories

> **Audience:**
> The primary audience is the client or witness; the secondary audience is the opposing lawyer.
>
> **Purpose:**
> To gather factual information.

Written interrogatories, requiring written responses, follow much the same procedures, but they require questions designed to close all loopholes. Because of this, they take on the flavor of "statutory language" in their preciseness. Because the attorney will not be present when the party writes the response and can't follow up on the answers, the questions should be phrased in specific enough language to elicit the needed information. Often that means asking the same question in different ways, anticipating the reader's possible misunderstanding or deliberate sidestepping of the issue. For example, these questions are from the interrogatory sent to Jan Wharton. In this *written* version, the questions require specific answers that will definitely fulfill the attorney's purpose to obtain as much factual information as possible. Note the techniques Attorney Baker uses to emphasize facts rather than emotions. He begins with less precise questions and gradually pins down Wharton's answers. Even the length of Wharton's answers indicates which questions really work for Baker and which are too imprecise to be valuable.

Q: Please describe fully all communications between you and Nelson Rayman that relate to your satisfaction or dissatisfaction with any work performed by Rayman and/or his agents and/or servants at the premises.

A: Defendant Wharton was generally satisfied with work performed by Rayman and/or his agents and/or servants at the premises and cannot recall any communication of dissatisfaction with work that had been performed.

Q: Was Rayman at any time required to redo any work because that work was unsatisfactory?

A: No.

[Several questions intervene prior to this next one.]

Q: Were the plans for the renovation or the schedule for the renovation changed in any way at the time subsequent to September 1, 1983?

A: Yes.

Q: If your answer to the previous question is other than an unqualified negative, please describe fully each and every change in the renovation plans or schedule stating as to each:

  (a) the date of the change
  (b) the nature of the change
  (c) the identity of the person initiating the change
  (d) all communications relating to the change
  (e) the effect of the change on the compensation described in your answer to interrogatory number 17

A: Several minor plan changes or additions were made at Jan Wharton's request during the course of the renovations:

In March 1984, Rayman installed a skylight over the common area. This addition was requested by Wharton during one of her weekly site visits. Additional material costs were borne by Wharton. Additional labor costs were borne by Rayman.

In March 1984, Jan Wharton was reviewing supply receipts from Nelson Rayman and noticed he had picked up $3,000 worth of copper tubing and plumbing equipment. This change saved Wharton $2,100 in material costs, but it did not increase Rayman's labor costs.

Also in March 1984, Wharton urged Rayman to use lathe and plaster instead of sheetrock in the lobby walls. Wharton thought lathe was more fire preventive and more durable. After some disagreement, Rayman agreed to hire two plasterers for the work. Rayman's labor costs were consequently increased, but Jan Wharton does not know the cost of this labor. Wharton's saving in material from this change was approximately $400.

In June 1984, Wharton asked Rayman to refinish exposed hardwood floors rather than installing a floor covering supplied by Wharton. Jan Wharton does not know how much this increased Rayman's labor costs. The savings to Wharton from the unused flooring was about $250.

As you can readily see, the first question includes the vague words *satisfaction* and *dissatisfaction*, allowing Wharton to avoid answering directly. Baker has a similar problem in his next question when he uses the undefined term *redo*. When the later questions define the terms specifically, Wharton has to answer in an equally precise manner. Asking if the plans were "changed in any way" is more precise than the general "redo any work," and the request for detailed follow-up elicits definite information.

As these two versions of investigative question illustrate, if the writer knows the *purpose* of the document, and knows the audience, the questions can be phrased to accomplish the writer's goals. Once the attorney has gathered the facts of the case, the next step is to report them in orderly fashion.

Objective Reporting

One of the hardest tasks for a lawyer is to be objective. Arguing is inherent to the profession and becomes so habitual that most lawyers can't help but take sides on any issue. But some legal writing requires objectivity; the document's purpose is best served when the writer presents all sides of the question equally. Two such situations are the client interview summary and the fact statement from an office memorandum.

Interview Summary

Audience:
The writer.

Purpose:
To record relevant facts about the client's story.

The interview summary, usually written from notes taken during the initial client interview, is an informal document for the attorney's own use. When hearing the client's version of the problem at hand, the lawyer jots down notes or records the interview on tape and later summarizes the proceedings for future reference. In this instance, the audience is usually the writer, and the purpose is to record the client's story exactly so that the attorney can begin the investigation on a solid foundation.

Sometimes in larger firms or in law school classes, the senior partners (or law professors) conduct the client interview while the associates (or students) take notes and write the summary. Regardless of who writes the document, audience and purpose legislate an objective tone. If you are the attorney working on the case and you don't have the details straight, you won't be able to form trustworthy opinions about the legal issues. Arrogant writers who impose opinions too early must see little value in legal research because they form conclusions before starting the investigation. Another word of caution here. Even though the interview is fresh in your mind, don't be tempted to abbreviate facts to remember them later. Chances are you'll forget the items you omit or not be able to read your own cryptic notes. Take the time to annotate everything so you won't have to rely on your fallible memory.

"Facts" Statement from Legal Memo

Audience:
Colleagues in the law office.

Purpose:
To inform lawyers of the key facts important to solving the client's legal problem.

The second situation where you need to be objective is in the fact statement of an office memorandum. Here, too, the purpose is to inform rather than argue. Audiences for the memo are usually other members of the law firm who want to understand what happened so they can help solve the client's problem. If the facts are colored by the writer's subjectivity, the attorneys who read the statement have less opportunity to exercise their judgment.

For example, this excerpt from a fact pattern improperly uses words with connotations that definitely create sympathy for the plaintiff. The emotional words are italicized:

Defendant Jan Wharton owns an *old* warehouse building that she is converting into a residential-commercial complex. Plaintiff William Revere attended a party hosted by one of Wharton's tenants at the complex. Revere *unwittingly wandered* from the host's apartment into a separate section of the building that was still under construction. There were *no lights to be found* in that part of the building, and it contained a *dangerous* unguarded *pit.* Revere fell into the *pit* and was injured.

Not only is Revere the injured victim here, the decrepit surroundings conspired against the poor fellow. Compare the slanted version with this more objective passage:

> On July 23, 1982, Jan Wharton, the landlord at One Traverso Street, and William Revere were social guests of a tenant who was having a party. During the evening, Wharton said to partygoers that three apartments would soon be available and the guests should "feel free to look around." Revere heard this invitation and looked at two nearly finished second floor apartments that had open doors.
>
> Located directly off the main entrance, the first floor foyer was open and used for access to the second and third floors. The normally locked plywood door at the right rear of the foyer was open the night of the party. The renovation area, allegedly unknown to Wharton, had a dangerous hole. The unlighted renovation area had stud walls, was clearly undergoing construction, and had not been used by the building's tenants. During the party, while looking for the third apartment, Revere walked through the plywood doorway. After several steps he passed through a stud wall and eventually fell into the hole, sustaining serious personal injuries.

Obviously, the facts presented in this second passage are more objective than the first. Even negative facts appear: "clearly undergoing construction," for example. In order to use these facts as a basis for productive research, the writer has documented the situation as objectively as possible. She can now proceed to strengthen the positive aspects of the case and prepare a good defense for the negative aspects. Her objectivity serves a valuable purpose.

Analyzing

Audience:
Colleagues.

Purpose:
To test possible legal interpretations of the problem's components. What are the probable outcomes of the various alternatives open to the lawyers working on the case?

Generally, legal writers analyze the legal ramifications of a case prior to constructing a persuasive argument based on this analysis. It's easy to confuse analyzing and arguing because they are so often intertwined, but effective legal writers maintain the integrity of the analysis by removing any overlap between it and argument. Analysis requires a context. As any good scientist will admit, productive analyzing means separating something into its component parts and viewing each of these parts in relation to the whole. For lawyers, the law is the context, and the individual cases are the components. Legal analysis of any case has two levels: breaking down the case into its problematic components and relating parts to the larger legal context. To decide how to proceed with a particular case, attorneys view it from all angles, defining the legal alternatives open to them.

For example, attorneys analyzing *Revere v. Wharton* need to discover the problem's components and then determine how the larger body of the law applies to each part. What was William Revere's legal status when he fell into the unguarded hole—was he a trespasser or was he within the scope of his invitation as a guest? And how does the renovation contract Jan Wharton made with Nelson Rayman match the legal definition of an "independent contractor"? If Rayman was independent, then he is the one liable for Revere's injuries. If he was Wharton's employee, then Wharton is vicariously liable for Rayman's actions. These and other questions comprise the "parts" of the whole case that need to be interpreted in a legal context. The lawyer's first step is to define how many issues there are in the case and then determine how they relate to one another in the eyes of the law.

In legal analysis, let the information you gather stand on its own without editorial comment. If you have thoroughly researched case law, you need only match the facts to the law and step aside.

At this point in the legal process, you probably have formulated opinions based on solid evidence and clear reasoning. You've interviewed the client, taken depositions, objectively stated the acts, analyzed the law's application to the case, and can now draw objective conclusions with authority. In an office memorandum, these steps are separated clearly into sections: facts, analysis, and conclusion.

In spite of temptations to appeal to emotion, legal analysis is not the place to do so. Instead, you should maintain dignified objectivity and let the strength of your well-organized discussion support your conclusions and recommendations. In the "conclusion" section of an office memorandum, for example, you can suggest that certain legal actions will produce better results than others, based on unbiased analysis of case law. The key to writing good legal analysis is to present supportive *reasons* for every major assertion. By providing such support, you can indicate your "opinion," but you're not arguing for or against it. Instead, you're laying out all the pieces and showing the reader exactly how you view the case and why.

The audience in this instance is not hostile, nor are you trying to slant the facts to prove your point. For this rhetorical situation, pieces of the analysis should all be visible for the readers to inspect and agree with or disagree with according to the soundness of your logic. If the lawyers plan to work together on the case, obviously they need to trust your discussion as logical advice, not as an appeal to emotion. The following is an example of a strongly stated analysis, devoid of emotional artifice. Note the clear statement of alternatives open to the attorneys handling the case:

> Revere was not injured in a common area unless his belief that the renovation area was a common area was reasonable. Nonetheless, Wharton is potentially liable to Revere under the act and at common law on a common area liability theory in that she permitted access to and failed to warn about the dangerous conditions adjacent to undisputed common areas.
>
> If Wharton can convince the jury that she did not have reasonable time to inspect the foyer and safeguard the hole, or if she can convince the judge that common area liability is predicated on injuries in or dangerous conditions in common areas, she may avoid negligence. Further research is probably necessary to find persuasive premise liability authority on the negligent access theory and the time periods for reasonable inspection.

Although the writer has a definite negative opinion about her client's case (that Revere probably wasn't injured in a common area), she suggests a possible way to approach the Court on this matter (to prove that Revere's belief was reasonable). Further, she carefully explains defendant Wharton's probable defensive actions so that the attorneys can prepare appropriate legal strategy to deny Wharton success in these attempts. The tone is objective but authoritative in its conclusions.

Persuading

Audience:
Skeptical judge or opponent whose job is to find the holes in your argument.

Purpose:
To convince the audience that your position is more reasonable than any other.

This category of legal writing is perhaps more misunderstood than any other. The common stereotype equates lawyers and used car salesmen. Contrary to what many law students and many members of the skeptical public may think, legal persuasion is not the art of twisting facts to hoodwink the audience.

The art of persuading without resorting to propaganda takes any writer a long time to learn. Your purpose is to convince the audience that your position is more *reasonable* than any other, not more emotionally correct. It's essential to base your argument on logic, not emotion, or you will be working against your purpose.

Once you have carefully explored the legal options and have had colleagues confirm your opinions, you're ready to take the case before a judgmental audience. This may be a judge or an opposing attorney, but whoever it is will remain unconvinced unless you pull out all the persuasive stops. And that's often extremely difficult because most cases don't have a clear-cut solution; there are degrees of "rightness," and the judge will determine which is the most reasonable in this instance. Your job is to influence that decision.

This "facts" section from an office memo matched against the "facts" from a trial brief of the same case illustrates the difference between an objective version and a persuasively charged version of the same situation.

Excerpt from *Fact Pattern, Office Memo:*
While allegedly looking for an apartment, Revere passed through the open foyer doorway into the darkened renovation area. Searching for a lightswitch, Revere passed through the stud wall and fell into the unguarded hole, sustaining serious personal injury.

Excerpt from *Fact Pattern, Trial Brief:*
While looking for available apartments at the landlord's express invitation, Revere went through a door at the rear of the first floor common foyer that, he believed, led to common passageways and other available apartments. Unknown to him, there was a large unguarded and unlighted hole in the floor near the open door—a hole created during the ongoing renovations. Revere took several cautious steps in search of a light switch. Immediately beyond a partially finished wall, Revere fell into the unguarded hole, sustaining disabling leg injuries.

The dramatic rendition of the scene in the brief's version surely needs little additional comment. The careful phrasing obviously colors the way the reader will perceive Revere's actions, from transforming "stud wall" to "partially finished wall" to suggesting that Revere took "several cautious steps in search of a light switch." What reasonable person wouldn't do the same thing when confronted with such a darkened and potentially dangerous area? Of course, Revere's attorney is counting on the judge to respond exactly that way to those facts.

DETERMINING TONE

As you can gather from the preceding discussion, the writer must define the document's audience and purpose to determine the most effective tone; the three rhetorical elements are inseparable. How subjective will the audience allow you to be? Is it appropriate to be persuasive? Should you be harsh in certain parts of your argument, or would it be better to soft-pedal those sections? One clear rule applies here:

Relationship of Rhetorical Elements:
AUDIENCE + PURPOSE = TONE

For attorneys writing a legal memo or a brief, this rule means they must do preliminary analysis before actually writing. And it means paying special attention to the relationship among the three rhetorical elements.

Chapters 6 and 7 go into more detail on how to use persuasive language for effective written advocacy. For now, it's important to know that your tone controls the impact of your language on the reader. The more persuasive your document's purpose allows you to be, the more "charged" your language can be. As an example, the office memorandum's purpose is to analyze the client's legal situation, making emotional appeal dangerous. If a colleague depends on your memo to give a complete analysis of how the law applies to the facts in the case, your tone should be *objective*. That doesn't mean you can't take a stand on an issue; it simply means that your purpose is to suggest a legal approach, not to win an argument. For a good example of such tone, look again at the example on page 28. It suggests a definite approach while maintaining objectivity.

A trial brief allows you to use a subjective tone, *persuading* the audience by controlling the reader's response to the written material. Writing persuasively requires you to judge your reader carefully. If you *overdo* the emotional manipulation, you lose your authority. But if you sound convincing without seeming unfair, you hit exactly the right tone. For example, this passage is subjectively phrased while not going overboard:

> Given the numerous grounds upon which the jury could find in Revere's favor, defendant's Motion for Summary Judgment on Count II should be denied. A jury may fairly conclude the open door and area beyond were implicitly held open as common areas for Revere's use. Alternatively, the jury could find that Wharton negligently permitted foreseeable access from the common foyer to the dangerous hole. Not only could the jury find that Wharton had actual knowledge of the hole and open door; it could also find that she had ample opportunity to discover and safeguard the dangerous conditions. Finally, the jury could find that Wharton breached her duty to warn and instead issued an open invitation to disaster.

Here the attorney's strategy is to imply that his approach is undeniably reasonable. By cleverly organizing the paragraph and choosing words carefully, he succeeds in controlling reader response. His first sentence boldly promises "numerous grounds" on which the jury can find for Revere—and then he provides them. The rest of the paragraph gives specific grounds and uses the intensifying "not only . . . but also" sentence structure to give the impression of an undeniable number. Even the word choice "fairly conclude" adds to the net effect, creating a sympathetic audience. The clinching final phrase "open invitation to disaster" seals the reader's response. It's hard to disagree with such persuasive language.

As this example illustrates, knowing the audience and the purpose for your document allows you to connect the two by choosing the right tone. If you consider all three rhetorical elements before you write, your language becomes more efficient and to the point, and your total drafting time becomes shorter because you have definite goals in mind as you write. You are an informed and purposeful writer.

For example, Attorney Smith wants to express his research results to Attorney Green. Smith has thought through his material and understands it fully. In fact, he knows so much about the subject that it's hard to pare it down to a form understandable to Attorney Green. Green doesn't need to know all the information Smith has gathered; she just needs the material relevant to the case at hand. Green plans to use this information to make a summary judgment plea for her client.

Before Smith writes the office memorandum, he needs to consider the three dramatic elements intrinsic to his communication task: audience, purpose, and tone. His audience (Attorney Green) and the document's purpose (to clarify the summary judgment issue) determine what tone will best express his point. Because Green is familiar with the law, Smith needn't spend time explaining legal terms as he would do if he were writing for a client. And because Green needs to be informed rather than persuaded, Smith should not rely on connotative and persuasive rhetoric. To save Green time, Smith should include in the memorandum only material pertinent to summary judgment. The memo should be written in a form that allows Green to comprehend it quickly. For example, the following issue statement from Smith's memorandum goes through several drafts before he clearly focuses it instead of clouding the case with extraneous words.

Draft 1:

According to Texas common law, does Revere state a prima facie case that Wharton retained sufficient right of control, not only to the end result of the renovation project at One Traverso Street, contracted to Nelson Rayman, but also to the mode and method in which the details of the work were executed, so as to overcome Texas' strict standard vesting legal status of "independent contractor" as opposed to "employee" within the written contract?

Final draft:

Is Wharton, owner of the property under renovation at One Traverso Street, vicariously liable as an employer to Revere for the acts and omissions of Rayman, her builder:

a. Where, according to the renovation agreement, Wharton retained control over the sequence of the work, selected and supplied materials, and made monthly payments not related to work stages?

b. Where Wharton regularly exercised control during the renovation, both concerning the methods and manner of the work and concerning the hiring and firing of the work force?

Notice that Smith's final version gives the legal question first and then specifically lists the facts important to deciding the issue. From the first draft's muddled phrasing and imprecise language, Smith has pulled the central issue and featured it, allowing Green to see the specific facts in context of that major problem of law. The final version is well organized and easy to read, making Green's job easier.

If any of the three variables changes for the next document Smith writes, he will need to make different choices. If Green, for instance, were a judge, and if the document's purpose were to persuade, then the entire situation would change. That's why it's helpful to explore the roles these rhetorical elements play in the four types of legal writing. If you recognize the applicable category and the three elements prior to drafting your document, your prose will be more powerful and take less time to compose.

Before moving ahead to the next chapter on organization, take a few minutes to review the important preliminary steps in the legal writing process. Each of these provides you, the writer, with more control over your audience—and over the situation.

CHECKLIST: ANALYZING THE RHETORICAL SITUATION

1.   Allow enough time before you write to consider the three elements of the writing situation: audience + purpose = tone.

2.   Analyze your specific *audience* carefully using the ten questions in this chapter.

3.   Compare your specific audience to the four common categories of legal writers' audiences.

4.   Determine which of the four kinds of legal writing you're doing, and establish a definite *purpose* for your document.

5.   Given what you know about your document's audience and purpose, choose a tone that connects the two. Remember to write for the *reader*, not yourself.

Problem Solution

If you know Problem A is the issue statement from an office memorandum and Problem B is the question presented from a trial brief, the differences in their wording and tone become clear. In the first one, the audience is comprised of busy lawyers who read the memo to help them plan legal strategy for their client, William Revere. The second problem's purpose is to convince a judge that the case should go to trial, not be decided at summary judgment. By looking at audience, purpose, and tone, you should be able to understand the rhetorical reasons for the differences.

The issue statement (Problem A) presents the law and the facts in an objective and open-ended fashion. The purpose of the memo is to solve this problem. Because the questions presented have as their main purpose to persuade the judge to take the case to trial, the tone is subjective—definitely *pro*-Revere. In the memo, the attorney presents solutions to the client's legal problem; in the brief, the attorney suggests ways for the Court to solve the same problem. That's the main rhetorical difference between the two situations: in the first, the attorney has the power; in the second, he or she does not. (For further specific discussion of these examples, turn to Chapter 7.)

Chapter 3

Organizing the Document

Problem

The following is a preliminary outline for a legal office memorandum. Read it carefully, and pay particular attention to the organizational pattern. At first reading it may seem adequate, but look more closely. Does this outline define the argument and offer a clear roadmap through the analysis? Will it save the writer time in the later writing stages? Think about how the writer could have changed the outline to be a more productive step in the writing process.

Issue:

Whether, as a matter of law and based on the nature of the injury, attempt to recover in civil suit for Vivian Casterbank's alleged injuries, which include wrongful breach of her employment contract with South End Family Planning Clinic, Inc., humiliations, embarrassment, mental anguish, and damage to her reputation resulting from her wrongful discharge, as well as a disabling psychological condition causally related to her wrongful discharge is barred by the exclusive remedy provision of the Michigan Worker's Compensation Act.

Analysis outline:

A. Introduction: The Michigan Worker's Compensation Act (MWCA)

B. The Exclusive Remedy Provision §418.131 and §418.301

C. Application of MWCA to plaintiff's injuries

D. Case Law Applications: *Milton, Moore, Stimson, Pacheco,* and *Slayton*

Conclusion:

Since the decision in *Milton,* Michigan has repeatedly upheld that the exclusivity clause of the act does not bar an action to recover contract damages. Based upon this, Casterbank can most likely bring a successful breach of contract action. Although the rationale in the majority of the discrimination cases presented seems to support Casterbank's wrongful discharge action, the causes of action may be successfully distinguished by the clinic. Casterbank must show that employer misconduct is the basis for the discrimination exception. A claim for the nondisabling injuries will probably be allowed by the Court; and if allowed, successful.

Because *Slayton* is a recent decision and not yet contested, it will be up to the Court's discretion whether or not to allow Casterbank's claim for disabling injuries. If the Court allows the claim, however, it does not follow that it will be successful. The Court may make the opportunity to distinguish *Slayton* as unique.

The problem solution appears at the end of the chapter.

The most common complaint lawyers have about their own writing—or about other lawyers' writing—is that it is not well organized. Difficulty with organization is understandable because these writers must thread the facts of a case through a web of statutes, holdings, and *dicta*, avoiding entanglements while missing no relevant points. It's hard enough for the writer to get his or her own bearings in such complex legal detail, let alone clarify the situation for a reader. But that's the main function of legal writing: to clarify how the law applies in specific circumstances. Chapter 2 discusses how to determine your specific audience, purpose, and tone. This chapter shows you how to think through the organizational process and then how to indicate this pattern to the reader, thereby keeping that audience "with you" through the steps of your argument.

LEGAL WRITING AS PROBLEM SOLVING

Lawyers are primarily problem solvers. Their clients present them with legal dilemmas in need of solutions. The catch-22 is that there isn't an absolutely right answer, only arguments based on previously drafted arguments—all open to reinterpretation. In this always changing world of legal opinion, an argument becomes "organic": its structure and its meaning are inseparable. In other words, the *way* a lawyer puts together facts and law creates the solution. To be effective, the argument's shape must be readily apparent to the Court and to other lawyers. Every step in the problem-solving process should be clear and apply directly to the case at hand. If no one can follow the logic of a legal analysis, then the writer's grasp of the material is questionable.

In spite of this demand for logical continuity, lawyers often are so intent on presenting all the information they've gleaned from their exhaustive research that they ignore the need to organize the material meaningfully. These writers assume the reader is capable of connecting the pieces into a logical argument. But without a clear organizational plan, there is no argument at all, only assembled research notes.

At this preliminary stage, your research notes are spread out across the desk, and you face a blank sheet of paper or an empty computer screen. You have two tasks before you: to make sense of the material yourself and then to explain it to a potential reader. How do you begin?

The Issue Statement as the Controlling Idea

Before outlining or composing, you need to define the major issue and draft the issue statement. This statement should explain the purpose of your document because the reader looks to it first for direction. In many ways, the statement of issue is analogous to a lens through which the reader first sees the problem. Particular facts or rules may loom large or fade into the background, depending on the focus of the lens.

Drafting the Issue Statement

The easiest way to determine this focus is to think of your task in problem-solving terms. What is the problem you've been asked to solve? What is the primary legal question you need to answer before you can answer any others? In order to determine the prerequisite issue, first identify the primary legal rule that applies to the problem, then decide which facts become significant in light of that rule. The issue statement combines the two in the form of a question: rule first, then the facts. Remember, the issue states the question the analysis will answer, so its phrasing controls the design of the entire document.

The following examples show how two different writers phrased the same issue in their office memoranda on *Casterbank*

v. *The South End Clinic.* The first version is the weaker of the two, burying the legal rule at the end and suggesting no clear order for the analysis:

> **Issue:**
> Whether Casterbank may recover in a court suit different kinds of damages for different kinds of injuries, including contract damages, emotional distress, and emotional disability, or whether such damages are barred in whole or in part by the rule that worker's compensation is the exclusive remedy for workplace injuries, even though the damages are caused by allegedly wrongful or retaliatory discharge.

Contrast this statement of the problem with the following one, which places the rule first then states the facts.

> **Issue:**
> Does the exclusive remedy provision of the Michigan Worker's Compensation Act bar civil recovery for any or all of Vivian Casterbank's alleged injuries arising from her wrongful discharge, including: (1) lost wages and benefits resulting from the breach of her employment contract; (2) humiliation, embarrassment, mental anguish, and damage to her reputation resulting from her wrongful discharge; and (3) a disabling psychological condition caused by her wrongful discharge?

The writer of this second issue statement controls the organization of the memo by emphasizing the nature of Casterbank's injuries. She establishes the context first, beginning with the key legal problem in question: wrongful discharge and exclusivity as related to the Worker's Compensation Act. Then she indicates the organizational strategy by her direct list of the alleged injuries. The subsequent analysis will naturally follow this established theme: first an explanation of MWCA and then an application of the law to the various injuries. Note, too, the effect of the second version's emphatic beginning "Does" rather than the weak beginning "Whether" in the first. Directly phrased questions pack a bigger punch and command more attention than indirect statements.

One further suggestion about phrasing issues. You needn't present the question in one sentence, regardless of length. Try to be as concise as possible, but be clear as well. If it takes several sentences to clearly frame the issue, or if it takes a short list of major points, have the good sense to use them. Be careful not to blur the focus from the outset, thereby losing your definitive control.

OUTLINING STRATEGIES

Once you've determined the controlling issue—the document's "focus"—you're ready to take the next organizational step: outlining an argument that answers the questions presented. At this point, many law students groan and say they write best without outlines. Citing their success composing college essays at the typewriter, they scoff at the suggestion of an outline.

Ignoring an outline in legal drafting is like quarterbacking a football team without a game plan. It works fine for sandlot games, but not in the big leagues, where it counts. Constructing a solid argument from so much data requires a preliminary plan; no legal writer will survive without one. Legal analysis is complex enough without adding to the confusion by ignoring the need for a clear plan of attack. You need to decide on a strategy that will most efficiently present your solution to the problem.

Using Visual Aids to Organize Notes

One trick that might help you is using visual aids at this prewriting stage to see how the pieces fit together. A chart like the one on pages 42–43 quickly organizes your notes, allowing you to see at a glance how the research cases support Casterbank's various claims. The writer has simply filled in the grid with the facts from the four cases, placing *Casterbank* on the bottom line for comparison.

Once you have interpreted the grid's information, you are better equipped to translate the visual display into an outline for the document. An outline of your argument does the same thing the chart does: it shows you how the parts fit together and whether your organizational plan gives a balanced answer to the question. To construct an outline that really works for you in this way, keep three things in mind:

- Decide on an order for your analysis.

- Write your outline in complete sentences.

- Make clear the relevance of selected material.

Chronological versus Topical Order

Usually, legal analyses are organized chronologically or topically, depending on the focus of the issue. Chronological order illustrates how judicial doctrine evolved. Beginning with an early appellate case and following the Court's holdings through later similar cases, this kind of organization emphasizes the evolution of the law, the judicial intent, and the historical context of the doctrine. This is a relatively easy strategy because the order is predetermined. Nonetheless, you might create confusion by not using parallel structure for each section of the discussion. In other words, if you begin your chronology of the case law by first discussing appellate case facts and then applying them to *Casterbank*, you should maintain that order throughout the argument. For example, *Stimson* v. *Michigan Bell Telephone*/relevant facts/holding/application to *Casterbank*; *Pacheco* v. *Clifton*/relevant facts/holding/application to *Casterbank*; and so forth in the same manner. Establishing such a clear pattern sets reader expectations you should work with, not against.

This excerpt from a memorandum on the *Casterbank* case illustrates the value of chronological order to show how the pertinent law evolved. Note that the writer holds off applying these cases to *Casterbank* until the end of the discussion, allowing full explanation of each holding first:

> Michigan courts are not consistent in distinguishing the nature of injuries that are not compensable under the MWCA. In *Stimson* v. *Michigan Bell Telephone Co.*, 77 Mich. App. 361, 258 N. W. 2d 227 (1977), plaintiff was allowed to sue for discrimination, but was barred from civil remedy for her embarrassment, humiliation, and loss of esteem among her peers. The Court reasoned that those injuries were an outgrowth of her mental disability. Because the originating disability was compensable under the act, its sequels had to be regarded accordingly. Injuries "not incidental to the cause of action" were compensable under Worker's Compensation.

Worker's Compensation Exclusivity: Michigan
Nature of Injury Analysis

Type of claim and alleged injuries ➤ Cases ▼	Contract claim	Discrimination or retaliatory discharge (contract): contract damages	Discrimination or retaliatory discharge (statute): contract damages
Moore	———	———	———
Milton	(NO) Overtime, grade promotion, merit system violations	———	———
Stimson	(NO) Dicta		(NO) Discriminatory failure to promote and discharge: FEPA
Pacheco	(NO) Dicta	———	(NO) Job discrimination plus discharge: FEPA
Slayton		———	(NO) Gender discrimination, retaliatory discharge: Eliott-Larson Act
Casterbank	(NO) Breach of handbook	(NO) Breach of public policy	

(NO) = MWCA is not exclusive remedy

(YES) = MWCA is exclusive remedy

——— = Not applicable

Loss of professional esteem	Mental disability	Mental distress before and after disability	Mental distress during disability
(NO) Dignatory injury (false imprisonment)	—	—	—
—	(YES) Muscle fatigue, mental depression	—	
(YES) Loss of personal esteem	(YES) Mental disability	(YES)	(YES) By logic of holding
—	(YES) Mental disability	(NO) Discrimination injury	(YES) By inference
(NO) Loss of professional esteem	(YES) Mental disability (maybe dicta, but redemption agreement)	(NO) Discrimination (and retaliation) injury	(NO) Discrimination (and retaliation) injury
(NO) Loss of professional reputation	(YES) Mental disability: manic-depressive, anxiety reaction	(NO) If whistleblower or retaliation injury is like discrimination injury	(NO) If whistleblower or retaliation injury is like discrimination injury

Later, case law overruled *Stimson.* The Court, in *Pacheco* v. *Clifton*, 109 Mich. App. 563, 311 N. W. 2d 801 (1981), merged plaintiff's pain and suffering and other mental injuries with the compensated psychological disability during—but not before or after—his period of disability. A distinction was drawn between mental disability and mental anguish. The disabling injury fell under the scope of the act; the nondisabling injuries affecting the plaintiff before and after the period of disability could be grounds for a tort remedy.

The Court in *Slayton* v. *Michigan Host, Inc.*, 122 Mich. App. 411, 332 N. W. 2d 498 (1983), draws even sharper distinctions between mental disability and mental anguish, not culminating in a disability. Following the *Pacheco* ideology, *Slayton* does not bar injuries resulting from sexual discrimination because they are independent of any disability compensable under the act. *Slayton* extends *Pacheco* by permitting recovery for nondisabling injuries during the period of disability.

If Casterbank can prove that her mental distress is the direct result of wrongful discharge and not from a disabling personal injury, she will be able to recover under the rule for nondisabling injuries in *Slayton.* She might also be able to distinguish a period in which she suffered mental distress, but not mental disability according to *Pacheco.*

The clinic will want to maintain *Stimson* is still a good law, and Casterbank's injuries are "not incidental" to the cause of action; therefore, they are compensable.

As the example illustrates, chronological order works well for the writer who wants to show the history of a particular legal problem—in this case, the evolution of the current trend in awarding compensation for employee injuries. Nonetheless, most legal discussions won't fall into this category. The more common organizational pattern for analyzing legal problems is the topical order, or order by issue.

Topical order depends more on matching the issue statement with the organizational plan than on parallelism for clarity. Topical structure explores the relationship of the issue statement's parts to established legal rules. The stronger version of the issue question presented earlier in this chapter exemplifies how this works. It suggests an order based on the categories of injuries Casterbank alleges. By analyzing each type of injury's relationship to the MWCA, the attorney can draw conclusions about which are compensable under the act and which are actionable in civil suit. In this plan, the writer divides the major problem into subtopics, discussing each fully before moving on to the next. If you make sure your main point of comparison—in this case, the kind of injury—predominates the discussion, you won't create confusion. Unlike chronological progression, this plan is an imposed order you must clarify for your reader, but the results will be worth the trouble. When written clearly, topical organization is far superior to other patterns because it forces the writer to analyze rather than describe cases. For example, this lengthy chunk of legal analysis follows a topical pattern:

A. Damages founded in contract:

Case law clearly supports the proposition that Casterbank's wrongful termination contract damages are not injuries covered by the MWCA. In *Milton v. County of Oakland*, 50 Mich. App. 279, 213 N.W. 2d 250 (1973), the Michigan Court of Appeals held that the MWCA did not bar the plaintiff's civil recovery on claims including wrongful discharge arising from the defendant employer's alleged breach of the employment contract. The Court focused on the nature of the injury, reasoning that the MWCA's purpose was to redress "industrial injuries" and that "the distinction between industrial injuries and damages arising from the employment relationship that are contractual in nature is undeniable" *Id.* ____, 213 N.W. 2d 252. The MWCA does not cover "damages founded in contract" *Id.* Likewise, in *Stimson v. Michigan Bell Tel. Co.*, 77 Mich. App. 361, 258 N.W. 2d 227 (1977), the Court of Appeals permitted civil recovery for injuries of discharge and failure to promote. This recovery outside of the MWCA was allowed even though, like Casterbank, the plaintiff suffered mental distress that culminated in a disability. On the basis of these decisions, Casterbank's contractual damages are recoverable in a civil action

B. Recovery for total and partial disability:

Casterbank can recover for her total and partial loss of wage-earning capacity arising from her psychological condition exclusively under the MWCA. Section 418.301 (4) of the MWCA specifically provides benefits of disability—"a limitation of an employee's wage-earning capacity in the employee's general field of employment resulting from a personal injury"—whether it be total or partial. A mental injury such as Casterbank's psychological condition is a "personal injury" under the MWCA. See *Slayton v. Michigan Host, Inc.*, 122 Mich. App. 411, 332 N.W. 2d 498, 500 (1983); *Stimson v. Michigan Bell Tel. Co.*, 77 Mich. App. 361, 366, 258 N.W. 2d 227, 232 (1977). Such an injury is compensable under the MWCA "when arising out of actual events of employment" Mich. Comp. Laws Ann., §418.301(2) (Supp.1984). Casterbank's injury arose out of her discharge, clearly an event of employment. Thus, the exclusivity provision bars recovery for her disability as an element of damages in a civil action Mich. Comp. Laws Ann., §418.131 (Supp.1984); *Pacheco* v. *Clifton*, 109 Mich. App. 563, ____, 311 N.W. 2d 801, 806 (1981). (To the extent plaintiff suffered periods of medical disability, MWCA is his exclusive remedy.)

C. Recovery for claims of embarrassment, humiliation, damage to reputation, and mental anguish:

Casterbank's claims for embarrassment, humiliation, damage to reputation, and mental anguish present the harder questions of the scope of MWCA coverage. It is now fairly well settled that civil recovery is available for such mental injuries before and after disability and perhaps even during disability. In *Pacheco* v. *Clifton*, 109 Mich. App. 563, 311 N.W. 2d 801 (1981), the Court of Appeals considered whether the MWCA barred civil recovery for the plaintiff's various nondisabling mental injuries existing before a period of work disability and continuing afterwards. The Court held that civil recovery for such injuries was not barred by the MWCA, emphasizing that "[t]his is true, not only of those injuries occurring *prior* to plaintiff's disability but also as to those occurring *after* his disability" *Id.* ____, 311 N.W. 2d 806 (emphasis original).

The Court of Appeals' latest decision in this context is not entirely consistent with this aspect of *Pacheco*, however. Employing an analysis that distinguished injuries compensable under the MWCA from noncompensable injuries by identifying the source of the given injury, the Court in *Slayton* v. *Michigan Host, Inc.*, 122 Mich. App. 411, 332 N.W. 2d 498 (1983), held that "a victim of discrimination may bring a civil suit to recover for damages for any humiliation, embarrassment, outrage, disappointment, and other forms of mental anguish that flow from the discrimination injury" *Id.* ____, 332 N.W. 2d 500. The plaintiff's mental injuries were barred from civil recovery only if they resulted from a disability *Id.* ____, 332 N.W. 2d 501. Although the Court cited *Pacheco* as authority supporting these conclusions, the result clearly goes beyond the scope of *Pacheco's* holding.

In this sample analysis, the topical ordering of each legal problem clarifies the writer's view of the question. He answers the easy questions first and then tackles the harder ones. Beginning this analysis suggesting Casterbank can recover in civil court for breach of contract damages, the writer then proceeds to discuss Casterbank's other claims—disabling and nondisabling injuries—relative to the Worker's Compensation Act. The analysis is not ordered in chronological sequence, but instead proceeds via topic. For most legal discussions, this analytical method is the appropriate choice because it concentrates on the relationship of the law and the facts, rather than on the progression of court opinion.

No matter which organizational method you choose, make sure it is the best strategy for presenting your solution to the problem. Once you choose, you must stick to that plan throughout the document, so your method for choosing is important. Ask yourself whether you are trying to emphasize the law's evolution or whether your main goal is to explore the relationship of the law to a particular topic. The first is best accomplished with chronological order, the second via topical order.

Outlining in Complete Sentences

Why should you outline in complete sentences and not jotted categories? Writing in whole sentences demands that you think whole thoughts instead of half-formulated ideas. Legal writers often have a general notion of how to go about answering a question, but they soon discover at the writing stage that they don't have conclusive ideas. As a result, they have to backtrack, restate, and travel off on tangents because the boundaries of their arguments are not set. An outline of complete sentences shows you not only the clear progression of topics, but also the conclusion you have drawn about each one. Sentence outlines force completeness of thought in the preliminary stages, saving you time and energy in the long run. Here's an example of a precise and balanced outline of analysis. Note the complete statements, the clear supportive material, and the conclusion apparent in each section:

Analysis:
A. *Introduction:* This analysis applies the exclusive remedy rule of the MWCA—as defined in *Moore, Stimson, Pacheco,* and *Slayton*—to Vivian Casterbank's alleged damages and injuries. Are Casterbank's three types of injury compensable under the exclusive remedy rule?

B. *Casterbank's disabling psychological condition will fall within the exclusive remedy provision of the MWCA.*

1. The key language of the exclusivity clause applies to Casterbank's psychological condition.
2. Specifically discuss Mich. Comp. Laws Ann. §418.131 and §418.301.

[Transition]

C. *Casterbank will be able to bring a civil suit to recover for lost wages and benefits resulting from the breach of her employment contract.*

1. *Milton* complies with *Moore* to conclude that the exclusive remedy clause does not apply to breach of contract.
2. The holdings from *Milton* and *Moore* apply to Casterbank.
3. Casterbank's employment letter and employment handbook constitute an employment contract.

[Transition]

D. *The current trend in the case law suggests that Casterbank's claim for humiliation, embarrassment, mental anguish, and damage to her reputation resulting from her wrongful discharge will also be actionable.*

1. *Stimson* bars civil action for injuries "not incidental to the cause of action."
2. *Pacheco* overrules *Stimson*, drawing a distinction between mental disability and mental anguish. Nondisabling injuries before and after the disability are actionable.
3. *Slayton* extends *Pacheco* by permitting recovery for nondisabling injuries during the period of disability.
4. If Casterbank can prove that her mental anguish resulted from wrongful discharge and not from a disabling personal injury, she will be able to recover under *Slayton*.
5. The public policy exception to at-will employment may also allow Casterbank to recover under the Whistleblower's Protection Act.

Such an outline allows you to look at your analysis to see if it is balanced, logically sequential, and complete. If you have written complete thoughts at this stage, the actual drafting process will move more quickly because you have done your synthesizing of law and facts. The results are displayed on the page in front of you and *should be almost as clear to any other lawyer as they are to you.* If that is true, the rest of the drafting process is merely a fleshing out.

Clarifying the Relevance of Selected Material

Though it seems embarrassingly obvious, clarification will also save you time. Two common mistakes in legal writing are (1) the writer cites rule after rule, authority after authority, without specifically relating them to the facts of the case at hand and (2) the writer discusses the facts in detail and includes facts from analogous cases, but forgets to draw legal conclusions. To prevent falling into either trap, ask yourself at the outline stage why you're including a particular fact or rule. Make a note in your outline to explicitly apply rules to facts. For example, this paragraph nicely connects law to facts and draws a relevant conclusion:

> The courts have never considered breach of contract to be within the scope of the MWCA. Furthermore, the exclusive remedy bar does not apply to damages founded in contract (*Milton* v. *County of Oakland,* 50 Mich. App. 279, ____, 213 N.W. 2d 250, 252 (1973)). In *Milton,* plaintiff brought suit alleging violation of merit system rules and improper discharge that resulted in physical and mental injuries. Here the Court found the injuries to be contractual in nature and outside the scope of the MWCA. Therefore, if breach of contract can be established in the Casterbank case, the Court will continue its present course and allow her to recover in civil suit for breach of her employment contract.

First, the writer clarifies the legal problem (breach of contract), then the relevant case law holding, the analogous facts, and finally the application to *Casterbank.* Facts and law balance nicely in this example.

After checking your outline for balance, you've completed the first drafting phase. You know the question, the solution, and the best order in which to present the supportive rules and facts. It's essential to be as clear as possible on all three of these points before writing the first prose version of the document. The clearer you are at this stage, the fewer revisions you'll have to make later. You can reserve your editing time for tinkering with paragraph design and individual sentences, instead of rethinking whole chunks of information. You have a firm grasp on the material; now you must provide equal access for the reader.

GUIDING THE READER

An author of any functional document—prose for the purpose of making the reader take specific action—keeps the audience in the forefront at all times. A technical writer, for instance, guides an end user through the steps of a process; a business writer guides a department manager or a consumer; a legal writer guides attorneys, judges, and clients. You have to try to keep this audience "with you" the entire way through your document. At the organizational level, you have three basic tools for guiding the reader:

- statement of organization

- document format

- signposts

Statement of Organization

Usually placed in the lead paragraph of the analysis section, the statement of organization is a direct admission of your organizational plan. It states "up front" the solution to the legal problem and indicates the arrangement of the discussion. This direct approach sets reader expectations, creating a roadmap for the analysis. In other words, the statement of organization tells the reader where you're going and how you plan to get there. By so doing, you avoid writing a mystery story instead of a legal analysis and avoid keeping the reader in suspense until the final paragraph. As many senior partners in law firms will admit, withholding the solution until the end is a major problem among new associates. Leave the mysteries to Robert Ludlum and Amanda Cross. As a legal writer, you should state your solution first and then explain how the evidence adds up to that sum.

The following lead paragraphs show what a difference the statement of organization can make in a complex document. The first plunges into the analysis without an apparent plan.

In *Stimson v. Michigan Bell*, 77 Mich. App. 361, 258 N. W. 2d 227 (1977), the plaintiff alleged that, due to her employer's sexual discrimination, she was discharged and suffered an acute nervous breakdown, humiliation, embarrassment, and loss of esteem. In deciding an appeal to a lower court denial of summary judgment, the Court of Appeals identified the plaintiff's injuries as "compensable because they culminated in a disabling condition" *Id.*, 258 N. W. 2d 227, 232. In later cases, the Court altered *Stimson* by allowing common law action for nondisabling mental injuries.

Now watch what happens when the writer thinks about the reader's possible confusion and adds one introductory sentence. Suddenly the paragraph seems to make more sense because it indicates a clear reason for the discussion.

In a number of recent cases, the fact of disability has distinguished the MWCA compensable injury from that actionable in civil court. In *Stimson v. Michigan Bell*, 77 Mich. App. 361, 258 N. W. 2d 227 (1977), the plaintiff alleged that due to her employer's sexual discrimination, she was discharged and suffered an acute nervous breakdown, humiliation, and loss of esteem. In deciding an appeal to a lower court denial of summary judgment, the Court of Appeals identified the plaintiff's injuries as "compensable because they culminated in a disabling condition" *Id.*, 258 N. W. 2d 227, 232. In later cases, the Court altered *Stimson* by allowing common law action on nondisabling mental injuries.

As is clear from these examples, the writer who makes a good first impression is going to have an easier time convincing the readers of the argument's validity. No matter how accurate the logic is, if readers have to work too hard to understand it, they will resist. That's especially true when your reader is a busy attorney or a judge who wants to know right away what the problem is, what the solution is, and how you've organized the discussion. The statement of organization provides those answers and puts the busy reader at ease.

Document Format

The second guide the reader has is the design—the "format"—of the document. The way the prose appears on the page focuses attention on your important points and leads the reader to the appropriate conclusions. Formatting for legal writers means using effective headings and subheadings, providing numbered sections when necessary, and using spacing on the page to help emphasize the document's large-scale organization and the relative importance of the discussion's parts. Nothing is more frustrating for the reader than to have to wade through dense prose with no directional indicators or promise of white space in sight. For instance, look at the difference between two *Casterbank* issues discussed earlier. Notice how the second statement gives clear organizational signals.

Issue A:

Whether Casterbank may recover in a court suit different kinds of damages for different kinds of injuries, including contract damages, emotional distress, and emotional disability, or whether such damages are barred in whole or in part by the rule that worker's compensation is the exclusive remedy for workplace injuries, even though the damages are caused by allegedly wrongful or retaliatory discharge.

Issue B:

Does the exclusive remedy provision of the Michigan Worker's Compensation Act bar civil recovery for any or all of Vivian Casterbank's alleged injuries arising from her wrongful discharge, including: (1) lost wages and benefits resulting from the breach of her employment contract; (2) humiliation, embarrassment, mental anguish, and damage to her reputation resulting from her wrongful discharge; and (3) a disabling psychological condition caused by her wrongful discharge?

The first issue statement makes an enemy of the readers before they even begin to read. It is dense, offers no clue to its organization, and looks hard to read. The second one looks readable. Because of the numbered parts and the directness of the legal question, readers trust they can understand the point quickly.

The most common formatting technique for legal writers is the *heading*. If written as complete sentences stating legal conclusions, these underlined or italicized headings tell the whole story of your analysis in abbreviated form. A senior partner can glance down the page and get the gist of your argument or your discussion simply by reading your headings. They should be brief but conclusive—not too general or overloaded with detail. The reader is more likely to trust your analysis if you've composed definitive statements that include specifics from the case, rather than general descriptions of law. It's important to include specific facts and to phrase the headings as argumentative, not descriptive.

Compare the following headings from memoranda on the Casterbank case. Note how much more you know about the second memo's analysis—and how much stronger it appears—because of the well-focused headings:

Weak headings:

A. *The Michigan Worker's Compensation Act*

B. *Two Subsections of the MWCA That Apply to Casterbank's Case Against the Clinic*

C. *Two Conditions of Liability That the Courts Have Found Not Subject to the Exclusive Remedy Provision of the MWCA*

D. *The Michigan Courts Establish the Distinction Between a Disabling and a Nondisabling Mental Injury*

Strong headings:

A. *The MWCA Exclusive Remedy Provision Bars a Civil Action for Casterbank's Disabling Psychological Condition*

B. *Casterbank Can Recover in Civil Suit for Breach of Contract Damages*

C. *Casterbank Can Recover in Civil Suit for Her Nondisabling Injuries: Humiliation, Embarrassment, Mental Anguish, and Damage to Her Reputation*

The second, stronger set serves as a roadmap to the analysis and indicates the writer's confident control over the material. Combined with a clear organizational statement, these headings will suggest a tough, well-ordered argument. Your reader will have to work hard to get lost.

Another formatting element lawyers should pay more attention to is the way prose appears on the page. It's one thing to use strong headings, but it's quite another to use them so they *appear* strong. Underlining or italicizing helps set off primary headings from subordinate material. Indenting less important discussion also directs the reader's eye to the major points first.

Few lawyers realize that one of the most powerful writing techniques available is document design. As is so often the case, they realize how important visual effect is in oral advocacy but ignore the importance of a written document's visual effect. Most people find prose that is attractively presented easier to read and much easier to remember. For example, here's a memorandum section that's hard to read because the writer ignored page layout.

> A. *Michigan case law suggests that injuries may be bifurcated between MWCA and civil action.*
> This section explores the MWCA's applicability to Casterbank's three broad types of injuries: psychological disability, nondisabling emotional injuries, and contractual injuries.
> 1. *MWCA provides exclusive remedy for Casterbank's psychological disability.*
> Throughout the cases researched the core of the exclusivity clause remains constant: disabling injuries are compensable solely by the MWCA. *Slayton* v. *Michigan Host, Inc.*, 122 Mich. App. 411 ____, 332 N.W. 2d 498 (1983) 500, affirms the prior cases by holding "if the plaintiff alleges both injuries covered by the act and injuries not covered by the act, he or she must pursue the worker's compensation remedy for those injuries covered by the act." The problem is whether Casterbank's emotional injuries, not disabling in themselves, are injuries covered by the act.
> 2. *Nondisabling personal injuries may be actionable outside of the MWCA.*
> In *Slayton*, its latest—and broadest—applicable decision, the appellate court states, "a victim of discrimination may bring a civil suit to recover for damages for any humiliation, embarrassment, outrage, disappointment, and other forms of mental anguish that flow from the discrimination injury. Such claims are not barred by the exclusive remedy clause of the Worker's Disability Compensation Act because they are independent of any disability that might be compensable under the act" *Id.* ____, 332 N.W. 2d 500.

Now look at how much more readable the prose becomes when the writer formats the document:

> A. MICHIGAN CASE LAW SUGGESTS THAT INJURIES MAY BE BIFURCATED BETWEEN MWCA AND CIVIL ACTION.
>
> This section explores the MWCA's applicability to Casterbank's three broad types of injuries: psychological disability, nondisabling emotional injuries, and contractual injuries.
>
> 1. *MWCA provides exclusive remedy for Casterbank's psychological disability.*

Throughout the cases researched, the core of the exclusivity clause remains constant: disabling injuries are compensable solely by the MWCA. *Slayton* v. *Michigan Host, Inc.*, 122 Mich. App. 411 ___, 332 N. W. 2d 498 (1983) 500, affirms the prior cases by holding "if the plaintiff alleges both injuries covered by the act and injuries not covered by the act, he or she must pursue the worker's compensation remedy for those injuries covered by the act." The problem is whether Casterbank's emotional injuries, not disabling in themselves, are injuries covered by the act.

2. *Nondisabling personal injuries may be actionable outside of the MWCA.*

In *Slayton,* its latest—and broadest—applicable decision, the appellate court states, "a victim of discrimination may bring a civil suit to recover for damages for any humiliation, embarrassment, outrage, disappointment, and other forms of mental anguish that flow from the discrimination injury. Such claims are not barred by the exclusive remedy clause of the Worker's Disability Compensation Act because they are independent of any disability that might be compensable under the act" *Id.* ___, 332 N. W. 2d 500.

The lawyer who has to follow set legal forms for writing documents can take advantage of formatting by not missing any opportunity to present information *visually* using charts, tables, diagrams, and lists. To put something in tabulation form means to present it in a systematic, highly ordered fashion. For most writers, tabulation means presenting material in parallel lists.

Quick Review

Parallelism means tightening your writing by using the same grammatical form when you present a list. Each item in the list is "parallel" to the others, thus creating a pattern that's easy to read. For instance, Julius Caesar said, "I came, I saw, I conquered." He didn't use the unparallel version: "I came, I saw, I decided to conquer." Look for opportunities to present your material in parallel structure, whether you choose to number each item or simply put a comma or semicolon between them.

Any document becomes more readily understandable when parts of it appear in short, easy-to-read lists. In fact, the more complex the material, the better such a simple structure works. For instance, read the following two versions of the same information. Which is easier to read?

> Michigan's *Whistleblower's Protection Act*, Mich. Comp. Laws Ann. §15.361 et seq. (Supp. 1984), provides a cause of action against employers for retaliatory employment discrimination against employees who have reported, or are about to report, their employer's suspected violation of law to public authorities. In order to recover under the act, Casterbank must show the threat made to her by Dr. Kaplan and her subsequent discharge from the clinic, and she must also prove that their actions were in retaliation for her threat to report them. In addition, she must produce convincing evidence that she was "about to report" them to a state authority for violating a state law. She must finally show that, as a result of these retaliatory actions, she has sustained her injuries.

Now compare this version, in tabulation form:

> Michigan's *Whistleblower's Protection Act*, Mich. Comp. Laws Ann. §15.361 et seq. (Supp. 1984), provides a cause of action against employers for retaliatory employment discrimination against employees who have reported, or are about to report, their employer's suspected violation of law to public authorities. In order to recover under the act, Casterbank must show:
>
> 1. that Dr. Kaplan threatened her and the clinic discharged her
> 2. that their actions were in retaliation for her threat to report them
> 3. clear and convincing evidence that she was "about to report" to a state authority
> 4. that what she was about to report was a suspected violation of state law
> 5. that her injuries resulted from Dr. Kaplan and the clinic's retaliatory actions

Notice how the second version pulls the complicated material out of the dense prose and arranges it in a legible list, permitting you to comprehend each section quickly and clearly. This design technique simplifies complex information that your reader would otherwise have to plod through.

Another design technique you can use to make your documents more readable is the visual aid. Charts and graphs, when applicable, definitely add to the effect your prose has on the reader. These graphic elements also serve as a subtle method for you to repeat information. That's why any visual you include should be keyed to the text, further explaining or illustrating a concept from the discussion. If your chart is clearly labeled and well designed, it can show the reader at a glance what your prose may take twice as long to show. For example, the accompanying charts (see pages 58–59) will be included in an office memorandum discussing the clinic's liability to Vivian Casterbank for wrongful discharge. They easily clarify the complicated analysis of liability issues.

This visual aid is an evaluation of the clinic's liability to Casterbank for violating the Whistleblower's Protection Act or the public policy of the WPA. Attorney Baker designed the "decision tree" to express four different issues involved in evaluating the clinic's liability under the WPA: (1) Did Casterbank honestly suspect a violation of the law? (2) Was Casterbank about to report the clinic? (3) If she was not about to report, is Casterbank's internal threat to report the clinic protected by the WPA's public policy? (4) Was Casterbank's threat to report the clinic a determinative factor in her discharge? In his analysis of the WPA, Baker concluded (1) that these issues were legal and factually determinative, (2) that these issues would be separately decided by a judge or jury, and thus, (3) that each issue should be separately evaluated.

Attorney Baker next wrote down shorthand reasons for and against each of the issues, drawing mostly on his memoranda on liability under the WPA and under its public policy. As to each issue, he assigned his best estimate of how the issue would be decided, expressed as a percentage for favorable resolution for Casterbank and a percentage for unfavorable resolution for Casterbank. Finally, Baker multiplied the probability on each branch to get overall predictions of winning and losing.

As exemplified by this chart, visual aids also permit the reader to see at a glance how the various parts relate to one another. A prose description of this same material would take much more space, and the reader would take longer to decipher it. Sometimes a picture *is* worth a thousand words, but visuals should complement the other techniques you use to guide the

**Evaluating the Clinic's Liability under the Whistleblower's Protection Act
and under the Public Policy of the Act**

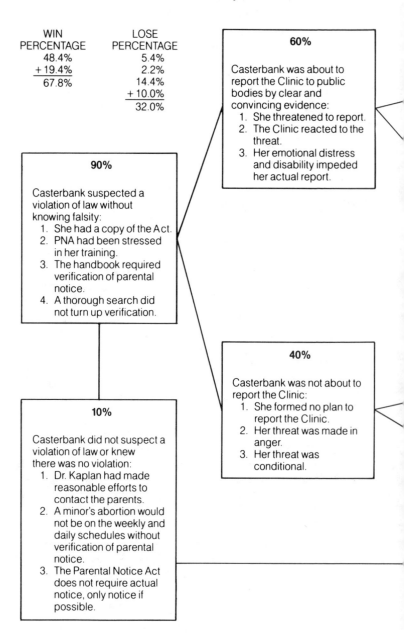

WIN PERCENTAGE	LOSE PERCENTAGE
48.4%	5.4%
+ 19.4%	2.2%
67.8%	14.4%
	+ 10.0%
	32.0%

60%

Casterbank was about to report the Clinic to public bodies by clear and convincing evidence:
1. She threatened to report.
2. The Clinic reacted to the threat.
3. Her emotional distress and disability impeded her actual report.

90%

Casterbank suspected a violation of law without knowing falsity:
1. She had a copy of the Act.
2. PNA had been stressed in her training.
3. The handbook required verification of parental notice.
4. A thorough search did not turn up verification.

40%

Casterbank was not about to report the Clinic:
1. She formed no plan to report the Clinic.
2. Her threat was made in anger.
3. Her threat was conditional.

10%

Casterbank did not suspect a violation of law or knew there was no violation:
1. Dr. Kaplan had made reasonable efforts to contact the parents.
2. A minor's abortion would not be on the weekly and daily schedules without verification of parental notice.
3. The Parental Notice Act does not require actual notice, only notice if possible.

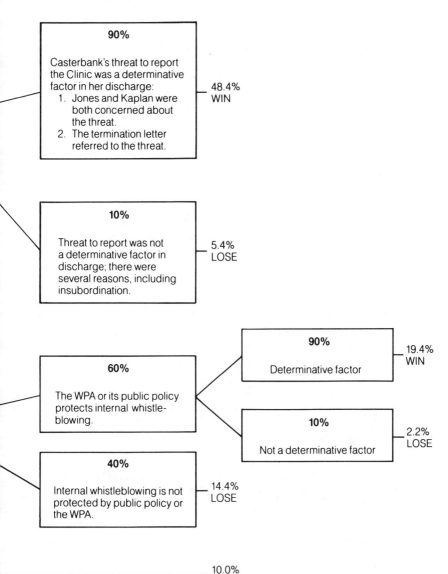

reader, not replace them. Your prose should offer directional signals as well.

One word of caution: as with any effective technique, you should use visual aids discriminately. Too much of a good thing ruins the effect. It's helpful to see lists, tables, charts, and other graphics in legal documents because they make the prose more comprehensible. The danger lies in using visual aids in place of carefully crafted prose. By substituting pictures for words, instead of using them to complement each other, you force the reader to write the plot the visuals illustrate.

Signposts

Unlike visual aids, signposts are subtle prose indicators that serve a purpose similar to graphic design. Because most readers can keep only a limited amount of information in mind at once, they need constant reminders of the larger picture. Signposts are periodic recaps of where your argument has been and where it's going. Even if you've used other guiding techniques, the reader's mind wanders during lengthy discussion and needs occasional refocusing. Signposts do just that: they direct attention back to the larger pattern, placing all the pieces in logical context once again. They also provide reflective pauses in the argument, allowing the reader to digest small units of information instead of becoming overwhelmed by the whole document at once. Finally, signposts every few pages allow you to follow the golden rule for debaters and writers: *Tell 'em what you're going to tell 'em, tell 'em, then tell 'em what you've told 'em.*

Written poorly, an attempted signpost sounds forced and lacks grace. Novice writers who have just discovered this technique sometimes use it much too blatantly, for example:

> Having demonstrated the broad applications of the exclusivity rule to all injuries caused by work-related events, this memo will now address Casterbank's individual claims in the light of the Court's application of the MWCA in similar cases.

Here's an example of an effective signpost tucked into an analysis of Vivian Casterbank's alleged injuries. It subtly indicates where the argument has been and where it will go without insulting the reader:

Unlike the language defining a disabling injury, the act provides no guidance on nondisabling injuries. Similarly, there is no explicit indication of whether contract damages are compensable under the MWCA. In the following cases, the Michigan Court of Appeals probes these two categories and provides the basis for analyzing Casterbank's contract damages and nondisabling injuries.

The key to effective signposts is to include them without the reader noticing they are there. It's an art to repeat information so subtly that it produces the desired result without seeming like an obvious repetition. Remember, you want to guide your reader logically through the argument, but a clumsy attempt at this can sound patronizing. No readers like to feel they are being led, but they're appreciative if you can gently point the way.

CONCLUDING

Most forms of legal writing have a separate "conclusion" section, giving you the opportunity to finish with flair. Strategically, the concluding paragraph is the most emphatic place in the argument because what you say here will be the chief idea the reader will carry away. Now's the time to confidently restate your position, trusting the rest of the document to support your logic. The audience likes to have the ideas put into final perspective in a clean, crisp fashion—it's a courtesy to the reader and an opportunity for you.

Elements of an Effective Conclusion

Some writers are so exhausted by the time they finish the legal discussion they are tempted to ignore the opportunity the conclusion provides. This is the place where you can say to the reader, "See? This is how it all adds up." You needn't go into detail because the body of your discussion has done that, but you should use the last paragraph or two to summarize the main points of your discussion. After all, the reader has been carefully thinking about your legal analysis and needs a quick review to pull it all together. Be brief—don't be tempted to retell the entire story. But express the major ideas once again, with conviction, and make sure you write so clearly that the audience can't miss the significance of what you're saying. Strong conclusions generally have four things in common:

- They summarize the argument.

- They are concise

- They are crystal clear.

- They carry conviction.

Take a look at this concluding paragraph, and check the author's use of the four elements:

> Based on case law, Casterbank can most likely bring a successful breach of contract action, although she may not bring a claim for her emotional disability because of worker's compensation exclusivity. A claim for the nondisabling injuries will probably be allowed by the Court. Because *Slayton* is a recent decision and not yet contested, it will be up to the Court's discretion whether to allow Casterbank's claim for disabling injuries.

This conclusion is adequate, but it lacks conviction. Although the first few sentences summarize the thrust of the legal analysis, the indecisive tone damages the value of the discussion. Instead of packing a punch, it dwindles to an end, adding almost as an afterthought that Casterbank's claim for disabling injuries may or may not be acceptable or successful. That's hardly convincing, nor does it suggest that the legal research has yielded definite results. The solution to the client's legal problem is vague at best. This is an example of how neglecting the confident tone can undercut exhaustive research. Readers hesitate to trust writers who don't trust themselves.

Achieving a Confident Tone

The previous conclusion sounds weak because it uses wishy-washy language: "most likely," "seems," "may be," "probably," "whether or not," "if," and so on. Words like these indicate that the writer is on the defensive and worried about guarding all flanks. It's a tough problem for a lawyer to write confidently when the law isn't definite on the subject. Nonetheless, there are ways to indicate the law's ambiguity and still maintain control of the situation.

The first step is to remember the advice given in Chapter 2: Audience + Purpose = Tone. Remind yourself about these rhetorical elements. In this case, you are writing an office memorandum to your colleagues to give information and recommend how best to help the client. Because the readers are not antagonistic, but require informative advice, your tone should indicate confidence in the legal research you have done. The audience assumes you have professional expertise; to proceed defensively belies their initial confidence in you.

The secret to achieving a confident tone is for you to trust your research and explain clearly the alternatives open to the client. No apologies are necessary. For example, the next conclusion allows for alternative solutions and even expresses some indecision, but the writer's tone conveys confidence:

> Michigan's case law has not yet met a set of facts that precisely squares with the Casterbank case. Nonetheless, some of her injuries are covered by the MWCA, and others are not. Casterbank's disabling psychological condition is compensable under the act and barred from further recovery; her breach of contract damages are more actionable in civil court. More open to question are her nondisabling injuries of humiliation, mental anguish, and damaged reputation. Based on available case law, Casterbank can strongly argue to recover in civil suit for these claims.

This concluding paragraph summarizes the argument, proceeds in a logical order, and packs a punch. Rather than using weak language to express the legal ambiguities, the writer honestly suggests where the courts have been indefinite by saying these injuries are "more open to question." Those words indicate the truth without undercutting the lawyer's problem-solving ability.

The next example is included to show how confidence can tip into drama—a danger all lawyers fall victim to occasionally. This writer becomes so involved in presenting her opinions that she moves from legal opinion to emotional judgment. Although most attorneys harbor such opinions privately, they are not appropriate material for the objective memo:

Although it seems absurd, Casterbank can recover for her minimal and inadequate contract damages, but not recover for her much more substantial disabling emotional injury. Through ineptitude and lack of disciplined analysis, the Court of Appeals has refused to resolve the issue of whether Casterbank should be able to recover for emotional distress and loss of reputation. Given the outrageousness of its discharge, one hopes the Courts would soak the Clinic for every penny it's got.

Obviously, the "forceful" tone this writer uses is inappropriate for the document's purpose—it's a definite mismatch among audience, purpose, and tone. Instead of working *for* the writer, this dramatic language actually works against her. Most readers will mistrust such heavily opinionated prose. Your goal is to achieve a tone that indicates confidence, not arrogance.

Writing a convincing conclusion is the final step in the large-scale organization process. From the initial stage, where the research notes are spread out on the desk, to this last paragraph might seem like a long journey, but not if you approach it systematically, keeping in mind the ten steps in the checklist.

CHECKLIST: TEN STEPS TO CLEAR ORGANIZATION

1.   Think of the task in problem-solving terms.

2.   Define and focus the issue (problem): rule first, then facts.

3.   Outline your analysis in complete sentences.

4.   Use chronological order to show how judicial doctrine has evolved; use topical order to clarify complex relationships.

5.   Put your solution first, then indicate how your analysis adds up to that sum.

6.   Write a clear statement of organization up front.

7.   Write headings in complete sentences leading to conclusions of law.

8.   Provide signposts for the reader.

9.   Choose the most effective format and design.

10.   Conclude confidently.

Problem Solution

The original outline has so many problems it will only add extra time and worry to the drafting process. The issue is backward, placing the facts first and ending with the law. The analysis outline has no sense of order at all. After reading it, you still don't know the writer's point or logical method, nor do the headings lead to any conclusions of law. To further weaken this outline's value, the conclusion is too long-winded and indefinite. It doesn't take a clearly supported stand on the issue—indicating the writer's probable lack of faith in the rest of the analysis.

Below is a much better outline, one that begins with a direct statement of the legal problem, shows the step-by-step analytical method for solving the problem, and ends with a short but definite conclusion. This outline will save the writer time in the actual drafting process because all the organizing work is complete.

Issue:

Does the exclusive remedy provision of the Michigan Worker's Compensation Act bar recovery in a civil suit for any or all of Vivian Casterbank's alleged injuries: lost wages and benefits resulting from the breach of her employment contract; humiliation, embarrassment, mental anguish, and damage to her reputation resulting from her wrongful discharge; and a disabling psychological condition caused by her wrongful discharge?

Analysis:

A. *Introduction:* This analysis applies the exclusive remedy rule of the MWCA—as defined in *Moore, Stimson, Pacheco,* and *Slayton*—to Vivian Casterbank's alleged damages and injuries. Are Casterbank's three types of injury compensable under the exclusive remedy rule?

B. *Casterbank's disabling psychological condition will fall within the exclusive remedy provision of the MWCA.*

   1. The key language of the exclusivity clause applies to Casterbank's psychological condition.
   2. Specifically discuss Mich. Comp. Laws Ann. §418.131 and §418.301.

C. *Casterbank will be able to bring a civil suit to recover for lost wages and benefits resulting from the breach of her employment contract.*

1. *Milton* complies with *Moore* to conclude that the exclusive remedy clause does not apply to breach of contract.
2. The holdings from *Milton* and *Moore* apply to Casterbank.
3. Casterbank's employment letter and employee handbook constitute an employment contract.

D. *The current trend in the case law suggests that Casterbank's claim for humiliation, embarrassment, mental anguish, and damage to her reputation resulting from her wrongful discharge will also be actionable.*

1. *Stimson* bars civil action for injuries "not incidental to the cause of action."
2. *Pacheco* overrules *Stimson*, drawing a distinction between mental disability and mental anguish. Nondisabling injuries before and after the disability are actionable.
3. *Slayton* extends *Pacheco* by permitting recovery for nondisabling injuries during the period of disability.
4. If Casterbank can prove that her mental anguish resulted from wrongful discharge and not from a disabling personal injury, she will be able to recover under *Slayton.*
5. The public policy exception to at-will employment may also allow Casterbank to recover under the Whistleblower's Protection Act.

Conclusion:

Michigan's case law has not yet met a set of facts that precisely squares with the Casterbank case. Nonetheless, some of her injuries are covered by the MWCA, and others are not. Casterbank's disabling psychological condition is compensable under the act and barred from further recovery; her breach of contract damages are actionable in civil court. More open to question are her nondisabling injuries of humiliation, embarrassment, mental anguish, and damaged reputation. Based on available case law, Casterbank can strongly argue to recover in civil suit for these claims.

Chapter 4

Controlling the Paragraph

Problem

The following paragraphs are taken from several legal memoranda and briefs. Read them with an eye for how their paragraph organization works for or against clarity. Does each of them cohere around one main point? Do they begin by promising to discuss that main point, and do they end having fulfilled the promise? How much work does the reader have to do to fill in the logic gaps between sentences?

1.   Michigan case law has carved exceptions to the general statutory rule of exclusivity. The court in *Moore* v. *Federal Dept. Stores*, 33 Mich. App. 556, 190, N.W. 2d 262 (1971), was the first to provide additional remedy for injuries not compensable under the act. The plaintiff brought a civil suit for false imprisonment to recover damages for humiliation, embarrassment, and deprivation of liberty. The act's conditions of coverage did not include the "gist of false imprisonment" or plaintiff's injuries resulting from the tort.

2.   An employee may bring a civil suit action against an employer for sexual discrimination. However, worker's compensation provides exclusive remedy for injuries not incidental to the cause of action and where they culminate in disability. If the injuries are incidental to the discrimination, they are not barred *Stimson* v. *Michigan Bell Telephone Co.*, 77 Mich. App. 361, 258 N.W. 2d 227 (1977). The court distinguishes between the tort of sexual discrimination and injuries stemming from the tort while it employs a merger system between physical and mental injuries and those that are disabling and nondisabling.

3.   In addition, we can argue that the renovations were incidental to the supply store, that there was a relation because Wharton wanted to get into the renovation business.

Hard, definitive evidence is not available, but the inferences we draw from the facts may create significant enough questions to defeat a summary judgment motion.

If Wharton is judged in control, then she is liable for the actions of Rayman in not barricading the hole and not locking the door; therefore, the case may proceed to trial.

If Rayman is judged an independent contractor, it will be difficult to prove the renovations were inherently dangerous.

The problem solution appears at the end of the chapter.

This chapter explains the whys and hows of paragraphing in professional legal prose. If you have difficulty controlling your paragraphs, this chapter should help you see the logic of designing strong prose units. As a by-product, your overall organization and your persuasiveness should also improve. Many writers believe paragraphing is arbitrary—they indent the text occasionally to appease the reader. Even the writers who do take paragraphing seriously can seldom explain why they indent where they do. When asked, they often fall back on the old standby: "It *feels* right to me." Lawyers suffer more than most from this problem because legal texts consist of interconnected arguments difficult to sort into paragraph blocks.

FOCUSING ON ONE TOPIC

As you probably remember from English grammar, each paragraph should have *unity* and *coherence*. Simply put, this means every paragraph should focus on one main idea—usually a subtopic of the larger discussion—and the sentences should link together logically. Although that sounds easy, it's often hard to recognize the boundaries of your main idea and to know how to present it as a unified block. In the following example, the writer has ignored cohesive unity and has composed an "unglued" paragraph:

> Not only did Rayman receive monthly payments that resemble a salary, but the defendant's company supplied all materials necessary for the renovation free of charge. Any substitutions made were in the actual course of performance, at times contradicting Rayman's previous plans. These indicia of control as to manner and method are significant in the North Carolina tests that determine the employer/employee relationship. Additionally, the defendant specifically directed the details of the renovation when she personally instructed workers to move panelling in direct contradiction to Rayman's previous orders. North Carolina considers an employer's control, or right of control, over manner and method the vital test in determining employer/employee status.

It's hard to determine this paragraph's main topic. Is it the fact that the defendant's company supplied the renovation materials? Is it the indicia of control as to manner and method? Perhaps it's North Carolina's test for employer/employee relationships? Or do all of these scattered ideas cohere under one major point not directly stated in the paragraph? Even though the attorney has achieved a professional tone and has apparently linked her ideas with transitional words (such as "additionally"), this paragraph lacks the glue to keep its ideas together. Before this prose communicates as powerfully as the writer wants it to, the writer needs to focus these thoughts for the reader so that the priority of ideas is crystal clear. Without sharp focus, too many thoughts compete for the reader's attention, creating the three-ring circus effect.

Avoiding the Three-Ring Circus

Attorneys often have to fight the urge to keep at least three rings in action all the time, making it hard for the reader to focus on one. From your experience, you know that when you're writing about a legal issue, you're often juggling so many ideas that it seems impossible to deal with only one at a time. Everything seems to overlap. Even more difficult for legal writers is clearly stating the major point of the paragraph, because such directness leaves you open for attack. But to write powerful prose, you must view every paragraph as a unified expression of a definite idea. You need to determine your point and risk focusing the reader's full attention on it.

To stand up under such focused attention, each paragraph must be inherently logical. If you establish a cohesive pattern for development in each paragraph, the whole document becomes easier to read because it moves in a series of logical steps. Your reader can concentrate on every major idea without too many ancillary thoughts vying for attention. To organize your paragraphs into focused units, consider these five suggestions:

1.   *Organize your material* deductively *so that your main idea is "up front."* For example, a paragraph about vicarious liability should begin with the main idea, thereby giving the reader a *context* for the rest of the discussion. Here is a simple first sentence: "Jan Wharton is not vicariously liable for Revere's injuries because the general rule in Texas precludes vicarious

liability unless the employer retains right of control of the contractor." From that sentence, the reader knows the paragraph
topic and expects a discussion of "right of control" to follow.
The purpose of the paragraph is apparent, creating a framework
for the point you want to make about right of control.

2.   *Write one sentence that directly states your major point.*
This direct statement goes beyond the introductory "context set-
ter" of Suggestion 1 and states the crucial point of the paragraph
(for example, "Wharton's acts of control were not sufficient
to transform her relationship to Rayman from employer-
independent contractor to master-servant"). This sentence is a
good example of a direct statement of the paragraph's point.
Every paragraph should have one sentence as direct as that one.
It may occur anywhere in the paragraph, as long as it's there
somewhere.

3.   *Use the rest of the paragraph to support and explain the
main point.* Make sure that you support your assertions with
sufficient explanatory material and check to make sure every
sentence *serves* that function. If you've included a statement that
doesn't support the main point, leave it out. Notice the lack of
coherence in these sentences: "Wharton was not negligent in
hiring Rayman. She exercised due care in selecting him, and he
was also known to be competent. Texas does not recognize renovation work as inherently dangerous. It seems clear that Rayman, not Wharton, is liable for Revere's injuries."

4.   *Vary paragraph lengths and sentence lengths.* Short,
choppy sentences create a disjointed impression, even when the
paragraph proceeds logically, for instance: "The court should
grant summary judgment for Wharton. It should be granted on
the negligent hiring issue. It should be granted on the dangerous
activity issue. And it should be granted on the control issue.
Wharton's acts of control are analogous to many Texas cases
decided as a matter of law. The acts of control are distinguishable from those cases not granted summary judgment."

5.   *Begin and end with transitional sentences indicating where
you've been and where you're going.* Here's the last sentence of
a paragraph: "If the Court rules that Rayman's legal status was an
independent contractor, Wharton cannot be held vicariously liable for his negligence." The first sentence of the next paragraph
neatly links to this idea while moving toward a discussion of

how the courts determine status: "Right of control over work details determines legal status in Texas."

Now look at how these five suggestions work in the following passage taken from a legal brief. Note especially how the writer proceeds in a confident and logical fashion, encouraging the reader's trust in such well-organized prose:

> The key element of the Texas definition of an "independent contractor" is the right of control over the manner in which work details are executed in a contracted work project. When determining right of control, the Court considers several categories of work details, but places the greatest weight on the right of control over basic employment decisions. An employer may control the final results of the contracted project without affecting an independent contractor's legal status.
>
> When determining legal status, the courts rely most heavily on contractual evidence. The Wharton-Rayman renovation agreement vests Rayman with the right of control over virtually all the work details, including control over employment decisions, clearly establishing his contractual status as an independent contractor. Further, Rayman explicitly accepts all liability for his negligent work or the negligent work of his agents.

Applying the five steps for writing a sound paragraph to this sample passage from a legal memorandum should allow you to see why these paragraphs are successful.

Emphasizing the Main Idea

Organizing the paragraph deductively is the best way to emphasize the main idea. Simply explained, deductive order means a pattern that places the major point first and then explains its relevance or application. In the first paragraph in the previous example, the writer first states the key element of the Texas definition of independent contractor and then explains how the Court applies this element to actual situations. In the second paragraph, the most important idea is that the Court relies on contractual evidence. Following on the heels of this idea is the explanation of how it applies to Rayman and Wharton's contract. Such a deductive order gives the reader a context for understanding the rest of the unit's argument—it's a pattern that is the opposite of the "mystery story" technique of some writers who love to keep the audience in suspense. Lawyers have no time for such mysteries; they need to know the point first and then the significant discussion of that point.

The two examples proceed logically from main idea to specific applications. A quick outline of the order verifies this:

Paragraph 1:
a. The key element is right of control over work details.
b. To determine this right of control, the Court places greatest weight on basic employment decisions.
c. The employer may control final results without affecting contractor's independent status.

Paragraph 2:
a. To determine legal status, the Court relies most heavily on contractual evidence.
b. Wharton/Rayman's contract establishes Rayman's status as independent contractor.
c. Rayman accepts all liability for his work.

In contrast, turn back to the disorganized paragraph example on page 69. Note that the first sentence gives no indication of the main idea. As the paragraph progresses, each sentence seems more and more random because the writer has provided no overriding context or framework for the discussion.

Weak paragraph:
a. Rayman received monthly payments, but the defendant supplied the materials.
b. Substitutions contradicted Rayman's plans.
c. These indicia of control as to manner and method are significant in North Carolina.
d. The defendant specifically directed the renovation details.
e. North Carolina considers the right of control the vital test in determining legal status.

Now look again at the stronger two paragraphs. Try rearranging the sentences in various ways to make another of the ideas more prominent. If the paragraphs are well written, as these are, such rearrangement becomes almost impossible because the order is so logical in the first place. Try the same thing with the weak example, and you'll probably have no trouble moving the pieces around. When you write your own paragraphs, make sure they pass this rearrangement test. If you can shuffle the sentences without disrupting the paragraph's meaning, you haven't used an effective deductive order, and you definitely haven't emphasized any point at all.

Assert / Support

As is clear from the previous examples, the best pattern for legal prose is to assert a point and then support it with either evidence or other explanation. Yet many attorneys, having worked through the details of a case, forget that the reader isn't as familiar with it as they are. These writers often assume that some assertions need no explanations. And some writers realize the need for support, but they don't link the supportive sentences together clearly, forcing readers to make their own connections.

Notice how the sentences in the stronger paragraphs clearly support each other as well as the main topic of the unit. Each sentence picks up on a topic discussed in the previous sentence and adds to it. If you look closely, only one sentence in both paragraphs links weakly to the preceding one, in spite of an attempt at a good transition word. The sentence—the final one in Paragraph 2—exemplifies an instance where the writer assumes the reader can see the connection. The previous statement establishes Rayman's independent contractor status, so the writer assumes it must be obvious that Rayman's acceptance of all liability for negligence further supports this status. But nowhere in the final sentence does the writer specifically express the logical connection. Instead, the reader must bridge the gap.

It's dangerous to leave such responsibility to the reader. If the sentence read, "Further supporting this independent contractor status, Rayman explicitly accepts . . ." the problem would be solved. Make sure every sentence you write hinges on the one before it, either explicitly or implicitly, so that it's impossible to misunderstand the connection. Be aware of the danger, and rely on your common sense to decide how specific you need to make the link.

This assert/support pattern operates on two levels: the overall organization of the paragraph should progress from major idea to supportive material, and each sentence should support the one that follows. Once you've mastered this pattern, two additional tips for paragraphing will make your prose more logical and certainly more readable.

First, vary your paragraph lengths. No reader wants to be lulled to sleep by repeating blocks of prose with no variation in size, and any reader resists a full page with no indentations at all. Before reading a word, readers are probably resistant to the dense prose. It's up to you to appeal to reader psychology by making your prose look interesting and readable, not plodding and dense. To do so, you'll need to compose some longer paragraphs and some shorter ones, but keep one rule in mind: don't repeat the exact same length twice in a row, even though you may be tempted to do so. Most writers get in a rut, whether they realize it or not, and begin to write paragraphs of the same length. Perhaps that has to do with the sense of tempo writers establish as they write, but any repeating rhythm without a break serves as more of a lullaby than a stimulus.

Second, begin and end with smooth transitions. That's such a large topic that it deserves a major section of the chapter all to itself.

WRITING SMOOTH TRANSITIONS

Every paragraph needs two transitional sentences: the lead sentence and the last sentence. These two serve as both the boundaries for the paragraph and its links to the rest of the text. Yet each functions in a slightly different way.

Lead Sentence as Bridge

Your first sentence is probably the most important one in the paragraph because it has two jobs to do. First, it must bridge the gap between the last paragraph and the new one. To do so, it should either implicitly or explicitly refer to the preceding material. The lead sentence from the stronger example's second paragraph illustrates this technique: "*When determining legal status,* the Courts rely most heavily on contractual evidence." That first phrase refers to the last thought in the previous unit, but it also pulls the reader into the new topic to be discussed. It isn't solely a reference to previous material.

The first sentence also serves another function. As mentioned earlier in this chapter, you should organize your material deductively to put your main idea first. That's the second function of the lead sentence: to introduce the topic of the paragraph. But you must be especially careful composing this sentence because you don't want to say everything in that one statement. If you get in the habit of explaining your whole thought in the first sentence of every paragraph, the reader will quickly begin to read only the first sentences. Such a pattern encourages skimming. You probably want your reader to follow your idea through all its supportive explanations, so you need to promise what the paragraph is about without giving away the plot.

This "bridge sentence" pulls the reader into the meat of paragraph by subtly asking a question that the rest of the paragraph answers. By no means does this sentence have to be in actual question form; instead, it should encourage the *reader* to ask the question. Usually, these unspoken questions are the common who, what, when, where, and how. For instance, the previous example—"When determining legal status, the courts rely most heavily on contractual evidence"—causes the reader to ask: "How?" The rest of the paragraph answers that question. If every first sentence elicits such a question, the reader will want to finish the paragraph to get an answer.

Here are a few more sample lead sentences that indicate what the previous paragraph is about and subtly raise questions about the main topic of the new unit:

Sentence	Reader's question
"The rest of the contract buttresses Rayman's contractual status as an independent contractor."	How?
"Although the renovation agreement allowed Wharton Supply Co. to provide work materials, Wharton made only three suggestions concerning work materials that Rayman actually employed."	What were they?

"Revere did not rely on ap-   On what did he rely?
pearances alone."

"In light of the *Hayes* test, the   How?
defendant retained control
over the manner of Rayman's
work."

Last Sentence as Forecaster

Now that you understand the double function of the lead sentence, turn your attention to the final sentence in each paragraph.
Here's the place where you indicate what comes next. The last
sentence should contain the seeds of the next main idea, but it
should remain firmly attached to its own unit. In other words,
this sentence should not be a total change of subject—a topic
sentence "moved up a notch." Instead, it should naturally suggest
the direction in which you're taking the reader. As always, this
should be done subtly so your reader isn't patronized. Again,
look at the sample paragraph. The final sentence in the first unit,
"An employer may control the final results of a contracted project
without affecting an independent contractor's legal status," indicates direction. It's almost inevitable that the lead sentence of
the next paragraph will be about the Court's determination of
legal status. And so it is.

But it's so easy to write abrupt, less than graceful forecasters
that stick out like sore thumbs. Here are a few from novice legal
writers learning the art of subtlety:

As discussed in the following paragraph, the category of work
details the Courts consider key when determining legal status is
control over employment decisions.

To best illustrate the judicial doctrine that has developed, the
next section will analyze the Worker's Disability Compensation Act."

Another practical matter that might make the Court hesitant is
the problem of distinguishing and proving embarrassment, hu-

miliation, and other nondisabling mental injuries. This memo will now turn to this problem.

As you can see, each of these is an obviously forced transition. Mechanical techniques are most efficient when the reader is unaware of them. Once your mechanics begin to show, the machinery on the page may distract the reader and undermine his or her trust in you.

Those Tempting Transition Words

One sure way to let your mechanics show is to fall prey to the temptation of using transitional words constantly. Words such as "also," "however," "nonetheless," "thus," "therefore," and "additionally" creep into a writer's vocabulary and quickly become omnipresent. If you're too tired to compose implicit transitions, these "quick and dirty" explicit links seem like a good alternative. But from reading others' prose, you surely realize that such transitions look forced and resemble Band-Aids instead of careful surgical stitches. The best advice for those who habitually use transition words in place of implicit connections is to remove them totally for awhile until you break the habit and can use them again sparingly.

If you're not sure whether you qualify as an offender in this category, check your prose. Do you begin a majority of sentences with one word followed by a comma? Do you have a favorite transition word (such as "however") that you use whether it's needed or not? Do you create multiple opportunities to use the "first . . . second . . . third" pattern in your discussions? If you answer "yes" to any of these questions, you qualify. Your mechanics are definitely showing and are not creating the nearly seamless prose you intended.

Implicit Transitions

Using implicit transitions instead of explicit ones creates prose that seems more professional and polished than prose welded together via transitional words. *Implicit* as used here means the order is so logical that the reader understands the natural connections. Perhaps the easiest method for writing such internally logical material is for the writer to follow the "given/new" sequence. If the paragraphs proceed from "given" or already explained information to "new" information, the reader can more easily follow the train of thought. For instance, if you have agreed upon the basis for Wharton's defense, you should begin from that point and move gradually in the paragraph toward a new idea. In the following example, the writer begins by establishing the already proven material, then takes the discussion to the next natural step:

> A major thesis of defendant landlord's motion for summary judgment is that she lacked actual knowledge of the open foyer door and dangerous hole in the renovation area. However, Wharton knew of the extensive damage to the floor, and she knew for several weeks that Rayman planned to remove the rotten floorboards in the renovation area near the foyer. A jury might reasonably infer that Wharton thereby had actual knowledge of the hole and chose to disbelieve her self-serving assertion to the contrary. Similarly, Wharton had ample opportunity to observe the open foyer door when she entered the premises. Opportunity to observe is sufficient to permit the jury to infer that Wharton had actual knowledge of the means of access to the dangerous renovation area.

This movement from "given" to "new" permits the writer to focus attention on the reader's progress through the discussion. By following this sequence in the paragraph, the writer establishes a pattern the reader can appreciate and one that seems naturally comprehensible.

Crafting subtle transitions weaves your ideas together in a pattern that seems logical and forceful. It's difficult to argue with such interlocking prose, because it gives the impression of inevitable "rightness." That's not to say your writing style can substitute for sound thinking, but the style you use affects the reader either positively or negatively, regardless of your argument's quality. Paying attention to the first and last sentences in every paragraph, using transitional words wisely, and varying sentence and paragraph lengths will present any argument in the best possible light.

INTEGRATING LAW, FACTS, AND CASES

Finally, controlling the legal paragraph demands attention to analogizing and distinguishing cases. Most discussions of law center on how previous cases compare to the one at hand. In attempting to juggle the law, facts, and possible remedies of so many cases, attorneys often fall victim to hopeless entanglements. But some simple suggestions may help untangle the situation.

Analogizing and Distinguishing Cases

For many lawyers, analogizing a case means setting up a pattern like this: First give the legal rule. Then write a paragraph explaining how the courts handled a similar case. Finally, add another paragraph applying these holdings to the present case. This pattern is sound. As discussed in Chapter 3, the law should always come first, and certainly it's a good idea to explain the similar case before applying it to the one at hand. But the danger lies in the mechanical, overly simplistic method some writers use to achieve this pattern and in the failure to create a clear framework for the reader to understand the relevance of the analogous case.

For example, the attorney may present the analogous case in isolation, not mentioning its pertinence until after the facts have been given and the holding discussed. Such a presentation lacks context for the reader. Rather than describing the details of the analogous case and then applying it to, say, *Revere v. Wharton*, it's a better idea to first suggest why the appellate case is important and then to give the facts. By so doing, you provide the reader with a context in which to view these details. Otherwise, they exist in a vacuum. To effectively analogize a case, you should begin by giving the point of law that is in question, a brief description of the specific comparable facts, and then a *direct* application of the analogous case to the case at hand. Here are a few samples of effective analogizing that follows the more sophisticated pattern of explaining the importance of the comparison and then interweaving the facts of both cases:

> 1. *Lindelow v. Pete Kewit Sons, Inc.*, 174 Neb. 1, 115 N. W. 2d
> 776 (1962), a case involving an employee who was injured while

swimming at a company recreation facility, clarifies the distinction between licensee and invitee. The Court emphasized that a social invitation does not confer invitee status upon the visitor: "The real difference between a licensee and an invitee is the purpose of the invitation. If the invitation relates to the business of the one who gives it or for the mutual advantage of both parties of a business nature, the party receiving it is an invitee. If it is an invitation for convenience, pleasure, or benefit of the person enjoying the privilege, it is only a license, and the person receiving it is a licensee." *Id.* ____, 115, N.W. 2d 781. Thus, the Nebraska common law does indeed provide the *Revere* v. *Wharton* court with a clear construct for determining the level of care a landowner owes a particular visitor.

2. Not only were the door and renovation area not expressly intended for common use, they were not in common use by implication, despite Revere's idiosyncratic subjective belief. Only where Wharton gives a tenant or his guests reason to believe that a portion of the building is intended for common use may the area be deemed a common one by implication. See *Parsons* v. *Drake*, 347 Pa. 247, 250-52 32 A. 2d 27, 29-30 (1943). In *Parsons*, the owner of a hotel owed a duty to keep in reasonably safe condition the areas where visitors would "naturally travel" or the areas "apparently intended for . . . use." No such duty was owed as to areas that "the entrant is using for a purpose not reasonably to be anticipated and for which such portions of the premise were not designed." The plaintiff in *Parsons* was denied recovery for injuries she sustained when the hotel balcony on which she was unexpectedly loitering collapsed.

Similarly, Wharton did not give Revere any reason to believe that the plywood door or unlit renovation area were intended for common use. The door was plywood and thus temporary in appearance, as distinguished from other finished doors in the building. Therefore, the temporary door should not have misled Revere.

3. *Wright* presented the Court with a slightly different variation of the issue of changing visitor status. In *Wright*, the defendant allowed the plaintiff to enter the premises to buy scraps of material that were stored in a rag room. On every prior visit, the plaintiff had checked in at the office and then proceeded directly down a hall to the rag room. At no time did the plaintiff receive permission to deviate from this route. Nonetheless, on the day of the accident, the plaintiff wandered from his normal route in order to avoid an obstruction. In doing so, he fell into an un-

guarded elevator shaft in an adjacent room. The Court ruled that the plaintiff became a trespasser when he left the areas that were part of his normal business pattern.

The Wharton-Revere dispute, like *Wright*, provides a solid factual foundation for a legal determination that the plaintiff exceeded the scope of his invitation. Revere had constructive notice that his business invitation did not apply to the first floor renovation site, which was obstructed by darkness and ongoing construction.

Note that in each of these examples, the order is *deductive* in that the reason for the analogy comes first, followed by the details of the cases. And notice, too, the naturally sophisticated language used to apply the analogy. In none of these samples does the attorney repeat the simplistic statement: "This case applies to *Revere* in the following way." Too many lawyers use that hackneyed phrasing over and over again, until their analogizing and distinguishing sounds like a broken record. Remember to use the suggested method for comparing or contrasting cases; but vary the phrases you use to present the material, and be sensible about repeating exact patterns.

Controlling Multiparagraph Chunks

When lawyers introduce analogous cases into their analyses, they are faced with the problem of manipulating multiparagraph "chunks" of information, because the point of most analogizing takes longer than one paragraph. In between organizing on the large scale and controlling individual paragraphs lies this often overlooked organizational level: controlling "chunks" of legal prose. Although legal documents depend on the overall arrangement of the parts, they also include multiparagraph subsections expressing self-contained points. It's your job as a lawyer to write these complete subsections and connect them to the larger discussion. For example, a memo discussing whether landlord Wharton is liable for Revere's injuries has to include several small-scale parts. As you compose the document, it's helpful to phrase these parts as questions you must answer on the way to solving the larger issues presented.

Large issue:
Is Wharton liable for Revere's injuries?

Subissue questions:
A. Is Rayman an independent contractor?
   Is the contract determinative of the action?
B. Did Wharton control the work project?
   What are the indicia of control?

To organize these subsections, you must show the reader how these parts connect to each other and why they are important steps leading to the main solution. As discussed in Chapter 3, a good beginning indicates the overall plan, thereby giving the reader a context for the analysis. Second, if you've outlined your subissue questions in the order suggested, follow that order in the actual written document. This arrangement allows the reader to follow the legal steps involved in logical progression.

Three Approaches to Small-Scale Organization

Within each section, you need to organize the discussion so that it includes law, facts, and a relevant conclusion. How do you go about doing this? Small-scale organization generally follows three approaches, though these are not the only patterns. The next few paragraphs discuss these approaches and some examples. Although the examples are long, take the time to read them carefully. They are representative subsections from trial briefs in *Revere v. Wharton.*

Law (Rule) Applied to Facts of Case

In this instance, the writer decides the established law clearly applies to the case at hand. For this approach to work, the facts must be directly related to the legal rule, and the conclusion must be obvious, for instance:

> *The Tenement Buildings and Multiple Dwelling Premises Act and common law govern this case, and Revere has not demonstrated he is entitled to recover under either.*

> The Tenement Buildings and Multiple Dwelling Premises Act ("the act"), 68 Pa. Cons. Stat. Ann. §250.551-250.552 (Purdon), is applicable in this case because Wharton is the landlord of a multiple dwelling premises within the meaning of §250.551 (3) of

the act, and Revere is a social guest within the meaning of §250.552 of the act.

The act, by its terms, imposes the duty of reasonable care upon landlords who have retained control over areas of their buildings that are intended for common use. Here, there is absolutely no evidence that either the plywood door or the renovation area were intended for common use or, in fact, were used that way. Revere's injuries occurred in the renovation area, far outside of the common foyer. Because Revere cannot demonstrate that his injuries occurred in a common area, he cannot succeed in his effort to impose liability on Wharton under the act.

Further, even if Revere could demonstrate that the first floor renovation area is a common area, Revere would be unable to demonstrate that Wharton breached her duty of reasonable care. Wharton had no knowledge of the existence of the hole or that the door to the renovation area was open (Wharton's Deposition, p. 16, lines 28–29). Revere has failed to demonstrate that Wharton had sufficient time to discover the open door and hole, given her lack of knowledge of these problems.

Common law also imposes an identical duty of reasonable care on landlords to safeguard common areas. Given the lack of precedent under the act, case law alone can persuasively demonstrate the boundaries of Wharton's common areas and the limits on her duties.

In this "chunk," the writer applies the statute directly to the facts of *Revere* v. *Wharton* and concludes that Revere cannot recover under the act. This direct approach works well here and is easy to follow. Note that the final paragraph suggests the Court must turn to case law to define Wharton's common area duties. The promised discussion necessarily will go beyond the bounds of this "law applied to facts" analytical pattern, because it will include analogous cases. Here, the writer has indicated she will change her organization approach in the next section.

Facts of Analogous Cases Applied to Instant Case

A lawyer usually takes this approach when the legal rule is ambiguous in its relation to the client's problem or when the analogous cases present such strange parallels as to be undeniable in their application, for example:

Although the first floor foyer is a common area, neither the ply-
wood door nor the commercial renovation area were expressly or
impliedly reserved for common use by tenants and their guests at
the time of Revere's injury.

1. *The areas were not expressly intended for common use.*

   The plywood door and the first floor renovation area were not
intended for common use. The door and the renovation area are
not identified as common areas in any lease. In fact, the renovation area where the injury occurred is now a commercial space
that will be subject to a lease. Thus, the area will never become
one intended for common use under the defendant's control. *See*
Portee v. Kronzek, 194 Pa. Super. 193, 196, 166, A. 2d 328, 329
(1960).

   With the exception of one incident involving the moving of a
piano, Wharton never permitted her tenants to use the plywood
door or the commercial renovation area for any purpose, let
alone a common one. Accordingly, the door and renovation area
are not common areas by intention. *See Fay v. 900 North 63rd*
Street Corporation, 137 Pa. Super. 496, 9 A. 2d 483 (1938). (An
unlighted side door was not intended as a night exit.)

2. *The door and renovation area were not implicitly available*
   for Revere's unexpected use.

   Not only were the door and renovation area not expressly intended for common use, they were not in common use by implication, despite Revere's idiosyncratic subjective belief. Only
where Wharton gives a tenant or his guests reason to believe that
a portion of the building is intended for common use may the
area be deemed a common one by implication. *See Parsons v.*
Drake, 347, Pa. 247, 250-252, 32 A. 2d 27, 29-30 (1943). In
Parsons, the owner of a hotel owed a duty to keep in reasonably
safe condition the areas where visitors would "naturally travel"
or the areas that "the entrant intended for . . . use." No such duty
was owed as to areas that "the entrant is using for a purpose not
reasonably to be anticipated and for which such portions of the
premises were not designed." The plaintiff in *Parsons* was denied
recovery for injuries she sustained when the hotel balcony on
which she was unexpectedly loitering collapsed.

   Wharton did not give Revere any reason to believe that the
plywood door or unlit renovation area were intended for common use. The door was plywood and thus temporary in appearance as distinguished from other finished doors in the building.
Therefore, the temporary door should not have misled Revere.

See Borman v. *United Merchants' Realty and Improvement Co.,* 264 Pa. 158, 107 A. 682 (1919) (Without allegations of misleading placement or appearance, basement door should not mislead person looking for access to second floor.), *Felix* v. *O'Brien,* 413 Pa. 613, 199 A 2d 128 (1964) (Basement door should not have been mistaken for powder room door.). Plaintiff may rely on *Argo* v. *Goodstein,* 438 Pa. 468, 265 A. 2d 783 (1970). In *Argo,* a blind door-to-door salesman was allowed recovery for injuries he received when he fell in a construction area after he entered through a finished, unlocked exterior door. A plywood interior door could hardly be so misleading to a sighted person.

The renovation area beyond the plywood door was dark and without light switches. Therefore, Revere should have known it was not an area intended for common use like the other lighted interior passageways. In *Fay,* the Court found that an unlighted side entrance could not reasonably be considered an appropriate nightime exit given the existence of a well-lighted front entrance. *See also Felix,* 413 Pa. 613, 199 A. 2d 128 (Darkened basement stairway should have warned guest.). *Slobodvian* v. *Beighley,* 401 Pa. 520, 164 A. 2d 923 (1960) is distinguishable from the present case because there the owner knew of regular public use of his parking lot, which had an unguarded, unlighted hole.

Revere not only entered through a temporary plywood door into an unlit area; he also proceeded into the darkened area until he came to a stud wall. Clearly, this wall should have demarcated the boundaries of any interior passageway. More important, the stud wall indicated that the area was unfinished, unsafe, and manifestly not intended for common use. *See Parsons,* 347 Pa. 247, 32 A. 2d 27 (Plaintiff could not reasonably believe that the exterior balcony that collapsed was intended as the hotel's lobby or waiting room.).

Finally, Wharton's vague invitation that guests at the party take a look around at apartments in the building should not have misled Revere, who could be expected to proceed with some caution. The invitation was not specific enough to mislead Revere to believe that the plywood door would lead to an apartment. In *Felix,* 413 Pa. 613, 615, 199 A. 2d, 128, 129, the defendant's general direction that the powder room was "right around the corner" was not specific enough to mislead the plaintiff to believe that an unlighted cellar door led to that room. There, like here, the Court noted that the plaintiff should have discovered the cellar stairs by the exercise of her own common sense, *Id.,* 615, 199 A. 2d 130. In sum, because Revere's injury clearly occurred outside of a common area, he is precluded from recovery.

Arguing from caselaw, the attorney here has applied the analogous case facts to *Revere v. Wharton* and has aimed this analogizing toward her point that Revere was not in a common area when he fell into the dangerous hole.

Combination of Above Two: Rule and Analogous Cases Applied to Create New Focus

This is the most difficult approach, but also the most efficient. To effectively organize a discussion this way, you must first state the rule and then suggest how parts of various cases are similar to yours. In so doing, you are creating a new perspective on the rule; you are putting together facts and law in a way not yet established and are arguing that the new focus is sensible. Obviously, this involves more risk than the other two, but it also is the least repetitive and often the most convincing. This example is from Revere's point of view; the previous two have been pro-Wharton.

A jury could find that defendant landlord gave Revere reason to believe that the open foyer doorway and the area beyond were intended for his common use.

[1]introductory paragraph summarizing legal issues and Revere's argument

[1]By her design of the entrance foyer, by the open door leading off of the common foyer, and by her open-ended oral invitation, defendant landlord extended an implied invitation to William Revere permitting him to inspect the accessible areas of the first floor of the building. Because a jury could reasonably conclude that Wharton gave Revere reason to believe he could make common use of the open doorway and area beyond, the boundaries of the common areas of One Traverso Street are

in dispute. Accordingly, summary judgment is inappropriate.

²basic legal background; rule described in *Revere-Wharton* context

²Defendant Wharton is liable for the dangerous conditions in the common "passageways" of One Traverso Street over which she "retains control" 69 Pa. Cons. Stat. Ann. §250.552 (Purdon). Not only is Wharton responsible for expressly retained common areas such as the first floor foyer, she is also legally responsible for dangerous conditions existing in areas she implicitly held open for use of tenants and their guests.

³citation to supportive cases

³*Parsons* v. *Drake*, 347 Pa. 257, _____, 32 A. 2d 27, 30 (1943); *Bowser* v. *Artman*, 363 Pa. 388, _____, 69 A. 2d 836, 838 (1949); *cf. Argo* v. *Goodstein*, 438 Pa. 408, _____, 265, A. 2d 783, 786 (1970).

⁴the most important subrule defining common areas is described

⁴The essence of the implicit permission test was defined in *Parsons:* "A possessor of land is subject to liability to another . . . for such bodily harm as he sustains upon a part of the land upon which the possessor gives the other *reason to believe* that his presence is permitted or desired" 347 Pa. _____, 32 A. 2d 30, *citing* Restatement of Torts, §343, comment b (emphasis added).

⁵Revere's case applied factually to subrule

⁵Because the door and area beyond were immediately accessible from the main entrance to the building, Wharton's design of the building itself gave Revere reason to believe that his presence was permitted. As the defendant ad-

mits, the doorway and area beyond are presently common passageways, confirming Revere's assessment of the layout. [6]In a similar case, a basement door off an entrance foyer was found by a jury to be a common passage to a basement speakeasy *Portee* v. *Kronzek*, 194 Pa. Super. 193, ____, 166 A. 2d 328, 329 (1960). [7]The invitation to use the foyer doorway, implicit in Wharton's design, was reinforced by the door itself being open. [8]In both *Argo* and *Portee*, an open door was pivotal to finding an implied invitation. In *Argo*, a business invitee case, a blind door-to-door salesman fell into an open hole immediately beyond an unlocked door. The court noted: "Indeed by leaving the door open within easy access of the sidewalk, [the possessor] had issued [the salesman] an implicit invitation" 438 Pa. 265 A. 2d 786. Similarly, in *Portee*, authorities had removed the basement door during a prior raid on the basement speakeasy. The landlord did not replace the door, and the guest of a speakeasy patron was justified in traversing the open doorway.

[9]Like the plaintiffs in *Argo* and *Portee*, Mr. Revere was justified in relying on the open door as an open invitation. Revere's reliance was especially reasonable because other doors in the building had been purposefully left open by Wharton to facilitate prospective

[6]an illustrative, analogous case

[7]Revere's case applied factually to different subrule

[8]illustrative, analogous cases

[9]direct analogy

[10]Revere's case applied factually to third subrule

[11]restated argument

[12]substantive issue applied to summary judgment procedural standard

tenants' viewing of available apartments.

[10]Revere did not rely on appearances alone. Defendant landlord voiced an express invitation to Revere and other guests that they "look around" the building without limitation. "Looking around" necessarily means traversing common passageways. It also implies that open areas are open for inspection.

[11]Revere reasonably believed that he was permitted to "look around" and to use the open doorway and area beyond in his search for available apartments. The boundaries of his reasonable belief would define the boundaries of defendant landlord's implied common areas. Defendant landlord attempts to artificially constrict the common areas to the four squares of her own intentions. [12]Whenever the boundaries of common areas are in dispute, juries have always been the final arbiter. *See, e.g., Portee,* 194 Pa. Super. ___,166 A. 2d 330; *Bowser,* 363 Pa. 69 A. 2d 838; *cf. Slobodzian* v. *Beighley,* 401 Pa. 520, ___, 164 A. 2d 923, 924-925 (1960). Therefore, a jury should decide the boundaries of the implied common areas of One Traverso Street.

Note the combining of rules and analogous facts to refocus the judge's view of the *Revere* v. *Wharton* case. By skillfully manipulating both law and facts, the attorney has built a logical argument so neatly interwoven it's difficult to find any obvious flaws. Every aspect interconnects, creating the impression of a seamless argument.

IRAC: Issue, Rule, Application, Conclusion

The previous three approaches to small-scale organization make no mention of IRAC, the most commonly known pattern for legal analysis. Its omission doesn't imply that lawyers should abandon it; in fact, attorneys should realize at this point that the principles behind IRAC govern the three approaches, too. But novice writers sometimes get into trouble by repeating the IRAC formula for every minor issue, thereby creating a redundant pattern that really hampers the document's professional tone.

Repetitive patterns become a problem in legal writing. Although it's essential to follow clearly logical order, the formulae law students learn from their textbooks and from some of their professors become carved in stone, and the students never veer from these writing patterns. IRAC is one such formula: Issue . . . Rule . . . Application . . . Conclusion. This advice for writing about the law serves well as long as the attorney realizes that writing is a dynamic, not a static, process. Any writer who attempts to always use the IRAC formula will produce fill-in-the-blanks documents not unique to each legal problem. And ultimately such programmed prose loses vitality and definitely lacks the conviction so necessary to persuasive arguments.

However, good legal writers should keep the IRAC advice in the backs of their minds because it forces attention to all four of the legal writing essentials. Leaving out the application, for instance, creates a serious gap in the argument. And the issue should always be at the forefront of any discussion. The best way to use such formulae is to think of them as guidelines, not absolute rules, and your writing will reap the benefits intended without suffering the consequences of machine prose.

Controlling the legal paragraph is a craft well worth mastering. If you learn a few simple techniques, your writing will sound more professional and your argument seem much more convincing. The following checklist is a refocusing of the techniques for making your paragraphs more readable and more forceful.

CHECKLIST: WRITING COHESIVE PARAGRAPHS

1.   *Legal paragraphs should follow a deductive order.* Put the main point first, and then explain it with supportive material. This creates a context for the reader and prevents your prose from becoming a mystery story or an adventure in learning. Such organization greatly increases your argument's readability.

2.   *All paragraphs should have unity and coherence.* That means each paragraph should discuss only one subject, and all the sentences should link together logically. Remember, the links between the sentences should be clear not only to you, but to the reader as well. Don't trust the reader to make the connections.

3.   *The first sentence of every paragraph should promise what the paragraph will be about, but it should not be self-contained.* In other words, introduce the topic of the paragraph, but lure the reader into the meat of the discussion by creating a question the rest of the unit promises to answer. A beginning sentence that "tells all" is not a good first sentence.

4.   *The last sentence of each paragraph should subtly indicate where you plan to go next.* Although it should not be an abrupt change of subject, it should turn the topic toward a new direction while remaining rooted in the unified discussion of that segment. This is one of the most difficult tasks for any writer.

5.   *Paragraph lengths should vary.* Check your prose for long units followed by long units. If you were the reader, could you sustain interest in so much dense prose? Feel free to write short paragraphs, as long as you don't get in the habit of writing all short ones. Either extreme is dangerous.

6.   *Multiparagraph subsections should be organized to include law, facts, and a relevant conclusion.* Your approach should emphasize one of these patterns for small-scale organization:

- law applied to facts

- analogous case facts applied to instant case facts

- law and analogous case facts applied to create new focus

7.   *Don't become formula dependent.* Use IRAC or other patterns as guidelines, not definite rules.

Problem Solution

1.   This paragraph lacks both unity and coherence. It has no clear main point, and its sentences don't hinge on each other because there is no firm connection between the first sentence and the rest of the paragraph. Further, the paragraph seems incomplete in its discussion. It leaves the reader hanging.

2.   Because this paragraph is not organized deductively, it resembles a mystery story. In fact, this paragraph is made up of all supportive sentences without a main topic to support. The reader has no overriding context in which to understand each sentence. By organizing the paragraph in the way he has, the writer forces the reader to plod through each sentence once and then go back up to the top to try to determine how they all fit into a logical framework. The writer has yielded to the reader the job of determining the main point. In this case, there are at least two possible major topics: (1) exclusivity and (2) the difference between sexual discrimination and other injuries. Such a technique is not only inefficient, it's also dangerous because it gives the reader such interpretive power.

3.   Obviously, these paragraphs are too short. It's fine to write occasional short paragraphs, but this resembles a jotted outline. Either combine these short paragraphs into one longer one, or make each sentence the topic of a longer paragraph expanding on the idea.

Chapter 5

Editing Sentences

Problem

Now that you've focused on some of the large-scale problems attendant to legal prose, zero in on the problems at the sentence level. Read the following sentences (from legal memoranda) as many times as it takes to understand their meaning. Why do you think you have to read them through so many times before they make sense? One possibility is that the writers weren't thinking clearly; another is that they didn't take the time to edit the tangled prose. Try your hand at editing them to make their meaning easier to grasp on first reading. Each of these samples suffers from one or more of the five sentence-level problems discussed in this chapter. The following pages give tips for revising sentences like these into more efficient and powerful statements.

1.   In order to overcome the legal status of "employee-independent contractor" vested in the Wharton-Rayman contract, Revere must present sufficient evidence that Wharton exercised control over the mode and method of the details of the work executed to signify that there was an implied change of their contractual relationship thenceforth vesting "right of control" with Wharton.

2.   If Wharton has a duty created by the inherently dangerous nature of Rayman's work, or by his lack of using proper precautions associated with renovation, she assumes vicarious liability for a nondelegable duty.

3.   Assuming the Courts decide, as a matter of law, that Jan Wharton hired Nelson Rayman as an independent contractor, we must portray renovation as inherently dangerous work as performed by Rayman to impute his negligence to Wharton.

4.   Granted, in these cases, the Courts employ a liberal construction of the employee definition as a matter of public policy; but, in the absence of statutory authority, the determination of employee within the meaning of the act is to be determined by the application of common law torts.

The problem solution appears at the end of the chapter.

Once you've written a complete draft of the legal document—or finished one full section of it—the next step is to edit what you've written. Ideally, the first thorough edit comes when you have the whole manuscript down on paper. At this point, you've analyzed your audience, organized the material, and focused it with the audience in mind. In other words, you know what you want to say and to whom. Now you need to shift your attention from these larger organizational concerns to the specific sentences that compose the document.

Revising sentences for optimum effect is the heart of legal writing. Lawyers with the patience to do it have a distinct advantage over those who assume getting the research down on paper is sufficient, no matter in what form. In writing, as in any craft, extra care distinguishes the excellent from the mundane. This chapter provides the tools you need to give your prose that extra polish.

Legal writers face especially difficult problems at the sentence level, because there always seems to be so much information necessary to each statement. As a result, most legal prose suffers from long, tedious sentences filled with qualifiers and convoluted legal references. Part of this problem stems from the writer's inability to distinguish statutory language from plain English, but much of the problem comes from the attorney's defensive posture. In trying to protect all flanks, the writer often loses the incisive phrasing essential for controlling a discussion or argument. As demonstrated throughout this book, the legal writer's goal is to use the elements of good writing to achieve a confident tone.

Rather than dwelling on how to defend against a counter-argument, attorneys should think about a good offense and consider first the elements of a good sentence. This chapter first discusses the components of an effective sentence. Then it defines the five major problems legal writers have at the sentence level and suggests how to fix them.

WHAT MAKES A GOOD SENTENCE?

When readers think about what they appreciate in good sentences, probably four elements are primary:

- tone

- completeness

- focus

- rhythm

Here's an example of a legal sentence that includes a lot of important information but still meets the four qualifications of a good sentence. This is the issue statement from a legal brief:

> Could a jury conclude that Nelson Rayman was not an independent contractor because of the defendant's frequent communications with Rayman, her specific directions to hire and fire, her sequencing of the renovations, and her providing the building materials?

First, the *tone* of this sentence is not pugnacious or overtly hostile. The writer asks a genuine question naturally arising from the list of circumstances given. In this regard, the sentence is *complete* because it asks a clear question and gives the reasons for asking it. All the parts of the sentence are *focused* so that the reader can easily understand how they relate to one another. To do this, the writer arranged the evidence in a series leading up to the question, allowing the reader to move through the sentence in a step-by-step fashion, grasping each part before proceeding to the next. Finally, the sentence has graceful *rhythm* because its structure is parallel, legal context appears first, and its language is efficient and natural.

In the light of these four elements, consider this issue statement from an office memorandum written by a first year law student. Note how contorted it sounds in comparison to the previous sentence:

> Can it be determined as a matter of law whether Nelson Rayman controlled the manner and method of the renovation work at One Traverso Street, thus making him an independent contractor and absolving Jan Wharton from liability for injuries sustained by Revere, a third party lawfully on the premises, and even if Rayman performed as an independent contractor, could Wharton still be liable for Revere's injuries if she did not carefully select Rayman for this job or if the renovation work was inherently dangerous?

In this exhaustive sentence, the writer attempts to include all the relevant facts and legal terms that might bear on the case.

Though including all the pertinent material, he loses the clarity of the sentence itself. But the writer is not totally at fault. His professors and his T.A. have told him that he must consider all aspects of the law and make every statement legally inviolate—hence, the string of qualifying phrases and clauses. Further blame falls squarely on the examples available to the students: the volumes of professional legal writing in law libraries and law offices. For instance, the following sentence from an actual case appears in a textbook discussion of civil liability:

> For, if some limitation must be imposed upon the consequences for which the negligent actor is to be held responsible—and all are agreed that some limitation there must be—why should that test (reasonable foreseeability) be rejected which, since he is judged by what the reasonable man ought to foresee, corresponds with the common conscience of mankind, and a test (the "direct" consequence) be substituted which leads to nowhere but the never-ending and insoluble problems of causation.*

It's no wonder legal writers have difficulty learning to clearly express the principles of law. Models like this one encourage bad writing. To get to the root of the problem and find out why the author of that passage wrote it so poorly, and to discover why many lawyers have similar difficulty, you need to look at the way most attorneys compose their sentences and at the common problems they have with writing.

FIVE NOUN-RELATED PROBLEMS

A close look at what happens when a law student—or a veteran attorney—has trouble writing clear sentences reveals a common cause for such problems: noun dependency. Five of the most common sentence problems legal writers have are rooted in lawyers' addiction to nouns.

---

*Overseas Tankship (U.K.) Ltd. v. Morts Dock and Engineering Company, Ltd. (The Wagon Mound) Privy Council, 1961, A.C. 338.

Reasons for Noun Addiction

Law school steeps the students in nouns. From their first year of legal training, lawyers are taught to think in nominative terms, especially in abstract nouns labeling concepts rather than naming specific people or objects. Because of this thought pattern, many legal writers string together one abstract legal term after another, with little attention to verbs or other structural possibilities reflecting clear and interesting legal relationships (parallelism, for instance, or the step-by-step order exemplified earlier in this chapter). Even the longest legal sentences sacrifice all other parts of speech to the dominant noun. Certainly the previous example of professional writing illustrates this pattern. That one sentence on civil liability uses twenty nominatives to ten verbs, and only two of the verbs ("corresponds" and "leads") are strong enough to stand alone without auxiliaries, such as "must" and "to be," used to support the main verbs. The prime "movers" of such legal writing are abstract nouns, not verbs, a paradox at the base of many problems.

Specific versus General Nouns

Legal writers, especially novices, love to use abstract legal terms. Perhaps to sound more "legal," lawyers often use the general labels for people, actions, and concepts rather than using their specific names. For instance, you might say:

> According to Texas common law, does defendant landlord state a prima facie case by claiming sufficient right of control over the renovation project contracted to co-defendant, thereby overcoming Texas' strict standards for vesting legal status?

But that sentence depends on abstract terms—there are no recognizable people or actions in it at all. Instead, you could write:

> According to Texas common law, did Jan Wharton retain enough control over the One Traverso Street warehouse renovation project to make Nelson Rayman her employee rather than an independent contractor?

This version is clearer and certainly more memorable both to lawyers and to other potential readers. Only in rare instances when you are arguing matters of legal principle or statutory points are the abstract terms more appropriate than the specific details. Usually, the definite details ground your sentences in reality, making them more understandable. It's a false assumption, though a common one, that lawyers who read legal documents don't want to read plain English. But legal writers have more than their share of difficulties *writing* plain English. The reasons for that stem directly from noun-related problems.

In law school and beyond, most lawyers fall victim to five sentence-level difficulties that stand in the way of clear, direct communication:

- nominalization

- addiction to the passive voice

- overuse of the verb "to be"

- overly embedded sentences

- repetition of sentence structure

EDITING THE FIVE PROBLEMS

When you've finished your first draft of a legal memorandum or brief, the last thing you probably want to do is edit it. If you're like most writers, you're tired of the subject, have no objectivity about it, and want to turn your attention to something else. Ideally, you should be able to put the draft away for a day or two and come back to edit it later. But lawyers rarely have that luxury of time. Instead, you need to take a deep breath and plunge back into the document—this time concentrating on the sentences. It helps to have definite problems to look for, thus making the task more systematic and a little less arduous. The following five problems deserve special attention because they cause nearly all the writing difficulties lawyers have with their sentences.

Nominalization or "Nounism"

If you are conscious of avoiding abstractions, you will not overload your sentences with vague nouns. Neither will you fall into the trap of transforming verbs into nouns, a habit that lengthens sentences and further obstructs clarity. If a poor legal writer had written the preceding sentence, it might serve as a prime example of nominalization:

> The trap of transforming verbs into nouns will not often be fallen into, and thus the habit of nominalization, in which sentences are lengthened and further obstructions are placed in the path of clarity, is avoided.

In this version, the most glaring nominalization is the word *obstructions*—a noun created from the verb *obstructs*, a change that lengthens the sentence by at least five words. Good writers check the copy to see if they can rewrite in leaner form any noun or adjective containing the seed of a verb. For example, the sentence "A common theme throughout the four Virginia cases analyzed is the Courts' reliance on the legislators' intent" becomes "In all four of these Virginia cases, the Courts relied on the legislators' intent."

The following examples of nounism illustrate the major problem lawyers have with it. Each of these sentences can be made much more direct and concise by turning the noun or adjective back into a verb:

> 1a. Is "right of control" over work details the point of determination for legal status in Texas?
>
> 1b. Does "right of control" over work details determine legal status in Texas?
>
> 2a. The assumption of an excercise of control must be so persistent and the acquiescence therein so pronounced as to raise an inference that the parties, by implied consent and acquiescence, had agreed that the principal might have the right to control the details of the work.
>
> 2b. One party's exercising control must be so persistent and the other party's acquiescing so pronounced that the situation implies both parties consented to give the principal the right to control the work details.

Passive Voice

The passive voice is insidious in the way it takes root, compounds itself, and gradually strangles the life out of an argument. Simply defined, a verb is passive when its subject is acted upon by an outside agent: "Rayman's status will be determined by the Court." In this example, the status will not act, the Court will act upon it. Because the subject ("status") does not initiate the verb's action, the sentence is passive. Written in the active voice ("The Court will determine Rayman's status"), the sentence is more direct and more efficient. But writers thinking primarily about legal terminology are likely to move "status" to a position foremost in their sentences. In a few instances, the abstract noun legitimately should appear first, but in most cases, the sentence is clearer in the active version.

Because you are grappling with legal concepts, you naturally write your first drafts by linking abstract term to abstract term, a process readymade for the passive voice. The resulting argument is twice-removed from the reader, once by its conceptual nature, and once more by the passive construction.

A good edit will correct this problem. After you complete the "thinking draft" that likely contains a majority of sentences beginning with passive terms rather than active agents, a stringent edit prevents tangled prose, such as the following, from slipping through to the final draft:

> Specific aspects of the renovation work would be controlled by Rayman as clearly designated in the written contract entered into by Rayman and by the owner, Wharton.

A more direct version is:

> Rayman and Wharton's written contract clearly gave Rayman control over the specific aspects of the renovation work.

Naturally enough, new associates and first year law students are exploring this territory for the first time and often use the passive out of fear—fear of directness that sets them up as clear targets for attack. Another attraction of the passive voice is the writer's false impression that it sounds more formal and therefore more intelligent. Add to this the bad habit of using the verb *to be*, a verb that often sets the stage for the passive, and the reasons for the addiction to this construction become apparent. The following passive sentences and their revised versions illustrate the clarity and the conciseness of active voice:

> 1a. Anyone who is married or living apart from her parents or guardian and is self-supporting in a legitimate occupation is

defined as an "emancipated minor" by the Parental Notice Act (PNA).

1b.   The Parental Notice Act (PNA) defines an "emancipated minor" as anyone who is married or living apart from her parents or guardian and is self-supporting in a legitimate occupation.

2a.   Although Rayman supplied his own tools, materials were supplied by Wharton's Building Supply Company.

2b.   Although Rayman supplied his own tools, Wharton's Building Supply Company supplied the materials.

3a.   Traditionally, at-will employment in Michigan could be terminated at any time by either party. An exception has been recognized by the Michigan courts based on the principle that some grounds for discharging an employee are so contrary to public policy as to be actionable.

3b.   Traditionally, either party can terminate at-will employment in Michigan. But the Michigan courts have recognized an exception based on the principle that some grounds for discharging an employee are actionable because they contradict public policy.

Even though the active voice is usually a better option, sometimes the passive can be useful, especially when you want to downplay the actor's role in the sentence. For example, in a trial brief, the defendant's attorney may want to use the passive in saying "The plaintiff was hit by a car" rather than using the active voice and saying "The defendant hit the plaintiff with her car." Similarly, if you represent the South End Family Planning Clinic, you may want to phrase your sentence this way: "Vivian Casterbank was discharged for refusing to assist in a minor's abortion" instead of the more direct—and, in this case, risky—active version: "The Clinic fired Casterbank for refusing to assist in a minor's abortion." But in most instances, the active voice works better and suggests strength rather than weakness. Most writers fail to realize when they're writing passives, and their prose obviously suffers. The best rule to follow is to learn to recognize the passive and use it only when you really need it.

Overuse of the Verb *to Be*

Connecting legal terms creates a dependence on verbs such as *is, are, was,* and *were* to link the important concepts. In the following example, the writer unimaginatively links legal nouns with forms of *to be,* creating not only unnecessary passives, but lack-luster prose as well:

> Virginia courts recognize that the landlord's duty is coextensive with the invitation. The extent of the invitation has certain limitations about where the invitee is expected to go, and the area that is off-limits should be adequately marked. The conditions surrounding the renovation site strongly support that notice was given to Revere not to enter.

Removing the *to be* verbs more vividly focuses the paragraph:

> Virginia courts recognize that the landlord's duty coextends with the invitation. Although the invitation implies where the invitee may go, the off-limits area should have adequate markings. The renovation site's surrounding conditions clearly gave Revere notice not to enter.

Because the passive requires an auxiliary form of *to be,* excessive use of *is, are, was,* and *were* usually results in an outbreak of the passive voice.

These three potential problems—nominalization, the passive voice, and the verb *to be*—have a common solution. Because every sentence contains at least one verb (and most have more than one), their aggregate effect is powerful. If writers pay more attention to these verbs instead of concentrating primarily on nouns, they can improve clarity by at least 50 percent. The percentages improve even more dramatically when you correct two additional noun-related problems at the sentence level: strings of clauses and phrases and repeated sentence patterns.

Strings of Clauses and Phrases

Most persuasive legal writing consists of skillfully manipulated subordinate (dependent) clauses linking the major issues contained in the main clause. These grammatical terms may sound unfamiliar or intimidating to you at this point, but the ideas presented in this chapter are really quite simple. The quick reviews should help you understand the few grammatical terms necessary.

Quick Review

Main Clause—a group of words containing a subject + verb expressing a complete thought

Subordinate Clause—a group of words containing a subject + verb *not* expressing a complete thought

Phrase—a group of words used as a single part of speech and not containing a verb

---

Here, too, lies a potential trap for legal writers. In their attempt to include all facets of each issue, lawyers often embed several qualifying constructions within the framework of the sentence. In many cases, this method of subordinating information is efficient, but writers run the risk of stringing together so many dependent clauses and phrases that they obscure the important ideas. Unfortunately, much written law sets precedent for this awkward prose. Consider the following example—filled with strings of qualifiers—taken from the Michigan Worker's Compensation Act (Mich. Comp. Laws Ann. §418.131):

> "Employee" includes the person injured, his personal representative and any other person to whom a claim accrues by reason of the injury to or death of the employee, and "employer" includes his insurer, a service agent to a self-insured employer, and the accident fund insofar as they furnish or fail to furnish, safety inspections or safety advisory services incident to providing workmen's compensation insurance or incident to a self-insured employer's liability servicing contract.

The number of explanatory lists between the main subjects of that sentence (*employee* and *employer*) obscures the primary point. Rewritten in an easier to read format, the sentence makes its point more clearly:

> "Employee" includes (a) the injured person, (b) the injured person's personal representative, (c) anyone who has a claim resulting from the employee's injury or death.
>   "Employer" includes (a) the employer's insurer or service agent, (b) the accident fund insofar as they do or do not furnish

safety inspections and safety advisory services relevant to worker's compensation insurance or a liability servicing contract.

The revised version illustrates an important factor. Note
that efficient prose does not always mean shortened sentences.
Although you may need to reduce the number of words in your
sentences, writing's major goal is to communicate clearly. In some
instances, it takes more words in varied formats to increase the
readability, even if it means unraveling a tightly woven sentence.
The previous example shows the benefit of using lists to enable
the reader to grasp the concept with a single effort of mind. As
discussed in Chapter 3, reading information presented in a list is
easier than wading through long series of explanatory phrases.

Legal writers also often tangle their thoughts in this fashion
when they string together qualifying prepositional phrases. Usually, sentences containing these unnecessary phrases reflect the
writer's inefficient habit of thinking in terms of nouns rather than
verbs. When possible, you should use no more than two such
phrases in a row and should replace the possessive "of the" with
an apostrophe. In the following example, you can rearrange the
sentence to omit all seven prepositions by transforming them into
adjectives or by using the possessive apostrophe:

Original:
The issue of the case at bar was whether the exclusivity clause
precluded Kissinger from recovery through civil action when the
injury was inflicted by an intentional tort of the employer and did
not result in disability.

Revised:
The issue was whether the exclusivity clause precluded Kissinger's civil recovery because the employer's intentional tort inflicted a nondisabling injury.

Note that "the intentional tort of the employer" becomes
"the employer's intentional tort," a more direct and economical
statement. Similarly, constructions such as "recovery through
civil action" can be rewritten more efficiently by turning the
phrase into an adjective: "civil recovery," thereby transforming
another noun-based structure into a more concise expression.

Relative clauses (usually introduced by the pronouns
which, that, and *who*) cause similar entanglements.

Quick Review

A *relative clause* is a dependent clause offering further information about a noun. It is introduced by the relative pronouns: that, which, who, whom. For example:

a) The statute, *which became law in 1964,* applies to this case.
b) The facts *that are questionable* should be omitted.
c) Judges *who are new to the bench* often are tough adjudicators.

For example, the writer can reduce these sentences to leaner form:

Original:
The Court accepts that Revere, who was a social guest of one of the tenants, was not a trespasser on the premises of Wharton, who was the landlord of One Traverso Street at that time.

Revised:
The Court accepts that Revere, a tenant's social guest, did not trespass on the premises of Wharton, landlord of One Traverso Street.

Original:
The intentional tort exceptions that Larson describes in his treatise are inapplicable to the compensation cases in Michigan.

Revised:
The intentional tort exceptions described in Larson's treatise do not apply to Michigan compensation cases.

Original:
The rule, briefly stated, is that personal injuries that flow from an intentional tort such as discrimination are independent of any disability that is compensable under the act.

Revised:
According to the rule, personal injuries flowing from an intentional tort such as discrimination are independent of any disability compensable under the act.

One basic revising technique untangled all the embedded clauses in these sentences: transforming the clauses into appositives or into participles.

Quick Review

An *appositive* is a word or phrase that immediately follows a noun or a pronoun and gives more information about it. For example, "Jan Wharton, *the defendant*, took the stand."

A *participle* is a verbal adjective. In other words, it's a verb form that functions as an adjective. For example, "The *presiding* judge" takes the verb "to preside" and turns it into an adjective modifying "judge."

Although these parts of speech may evoke unpleasant memories of rigid high school grammar lessons, they are invaluable editing tools, especially for lawyers needing to compact a lot of information into each sentence. The "who" clauses in the first example easily reduce to appositives by dropping the unnecessary verbs: "*who was* a social guest of the tenant" becomes "a tenant's social guest" and "*who was* the landlord" changes to "the landlord."

In other examples, you can best focus the sentences by changing the "that" and "which" clauses into participles. For instance, "the intentional tort exceptions *that Larson describes* in his treatise" can be written more efficiently by deleting the relative pronoun and turning the verb into a participle: "the intentional tort exceptions *described in* Larson's treatise." Likewise, in the last example, the "personal injuries *that flow*" condenses to "personal injuries *flowing* from. . . ."

Options for Editing Strings of Clauses or Phrases

- Use apostrophes to indicate possession.

- Turn prepositional phrases into adjectives.

- Remove the verb in "who," "which," and "that" clauses, creating more concise appositives.

- Change the verb in "who," "which," and "that" clauses into an adjective (participle).

Again, the key to revising tangled prose caused by strings of clauses or phrases is to look twice at every relative clause and phrase. If it's possible to remove them, do so.

Repeated Sentence Patterns

Often this reduction process, though a positive step, results in a further difficulty. When you reduce each sentence to its simplest state, the prose may consist of many short sentences beginning with a subject + verb format:

> Nelson Rayman performed as an independent contractor at One Traverso Street. He controlled the manner and method of the renovation work. Wharton, the owner, controlled only the results of the project. Rayman carefully completed the renovations according to the terms of their unambiguous contract. He hired, directed, and compensated the workers. Wharton only determined the sequence of the renovations. She also supplied building materials for the project.

In this example, the writer has reduced the overweight constructions but hasn't paid attention to the reader's need for sentence variety. Without variation, the argument is difficult to read for reasons other than tangled structures or abstract ideas. The pendulum has swung to the opposite extreme: the prose has become overly simplistic. Not only is it a chore to read pages and pages of this redundant pattern, but the argument no longer sounds professional. Instead of interweaving the pertinent facts, the writer has listed them in choppy, isolated fashion, none specifically connected to any other.

To clearly integrate the facts with the legal ramifications of a case, you must carefully manipulate sentence structure. Varying sentence lengths, beginnings, and types creates readable patterns that suggest interlocking legal structures behind them.

Sentence Lengths

In writing, just as in any long process, repetition tends to set in. Sometimes writers unconsciously fall into the rhythm of repeating the same sentence length throughout a paragraph or a page. Although everything else in those sentences may be varied, the repetitious rhythm will have a negative effect on the reader. Analogous is the situation of the driver who begins to watch the repeating pattern of white lines in the road. No matter how stimulating the conversation in the car or how loud the music on the radio, the hypnotic effect of those repeating highway lines causes drowsiness. So, too, with lines of prose. To avoid lulling the reader, make sure each paragraph contains sentences varied in length. The rule of thumb is that every fourth sentence should be a short one—but such "rules" establish equally repetitious patterns. It's better to be aware of the need for variety and use common sense about alternating lengths.

Sentence Beginnings

In attempting to pare down overweight constructions, legal writers often take the extreme step of beginning every sentence with a straightforward but redundant subject + verb pattern. By so doing, they also lose the opportunity to subordinate ideas in introductory dependent clauses or to use other transitional devices indicating the exact relationship of the ideas in the sentence. Chapter 4 explains in detail how to use effective transitional devices to control the meaning of your paragraphs. For now, you should think about how the ideas in each sentence hinge on one another. Is it possible to directly indicate that link at the beginning of each sentence instead of starting each new statement with a disconnected noun followed by a verb?

Quick Review

Coordinate conjunctions (*and, but, or*) join sentence elements of equal value. For example, "The jury returned the verdict, and the judge passed sentence." In that sentence, neither half is more important than the other. The jury's verdict and the judge's sentence are of equal weight. But if the sentence read, "After the jury returned the verdict, the judge passed sentence," the first part can no longer stand as a complete idea; it's now dependent on the second part to complete its meaning. The subordinating conjunction *after* changed the relationship of the sentence elements. Subordinating conjunctions always indicate the nature of one element's dependence on another.

Here's a partial list of these conjunctions: after, although, because, before, since, until, when, while. Adding one of these subordinating conjunctions in front of a subject and verb makes the whole element a dependent clause.

For example, beginning the following statement with a dependent clause adds emphasis to the second part of the sentence:

> Although their contract clearly established Wharton and Rayman's employer/independent contractor relationship, the fact that their conduct was consistent with their contract determines Rayman's status.

Beginning with subject + verb and using the coordinate conjunction *and* gives the two halves of the sentence equal footing:

> Wharton and Rayman's contract clearly established their employer/independent contractor relationship, and the fact that their conduct was consistent with their contract determines Rayman's status.

Because most legal writing discusses intricate legal relationships, you should pay special attention to beginning your sentences in a way that indicates relationships, avoiding consistent subject + verb patterns.

Sentence Types

Just as repeating sentence lengths creates a dull rhythm, so does favoring one sentence type over the others. As long as you recognize your predilection for one pattern, you can vary the types when you edit the rough draft.

Quick Review

There are four basic sentence types: simple, complex, compound, and compound-complex. Here's a quick review of these structures, with the parts marked:

Simple = One main clause + any number of phrases

Main clause:
"*Rayman agreed to renovate Wharton's warehouse* within one year in accordance with the previously drafted blueprints."

Complex = One main clause + one or more dependent clauses and any number of phrases

Dependent clause:
"*While the renovations were in progress,*

Main clause:
Wharton made, over Rayman's objections, *four on-site modifications in the plans and materials.*"

Compound = Two or more main clauses + any number of phrases

Main clause:
"*Wharton could not terminate Rayman's employment contract at will,* and

Main clause:
Rayman was not bound by his contract to work exclusively for Wharton."

Compound-complex = Two or more main clauses + one or more dependent clauses and any number of phrases

Dependent clause:
"*Although Wharton probably gave Rayman full control* over the renovation area,

Main clause:
she relinquished partial control, and

Main clause:
this fact should allow her to avoid liability."

As you can see, to subordinate ideas effectively, you must use complex or compound-complex sentences. By so doing, you make it easy for the reader to see what is important and what is less so. The relationship of ideas becomes clear. In addition to manipulating clauses to show how your ideas fit together, you can also use other strategies to indicate the cohesiveness of your discussion.

EFFECTIVE SENTENCE STRATEGIES

Legal writers need to establish effective organizational techniques at the sentence level so that the order of information in these building blocks reinforces the overall structure. Emphasis and cohesion in a lawyer's written argument are reflected in the strategy of the individual sentence. Two main strategies serve legal writers well: the given/new contract and parallel structure.

The "Given/New" Contract

As suggested in the discussion of paragraphs in Chapter 4, placing known material first and new information—perhaps more opinionated or more emphatic points—at the end logically eases the reader from the familiar to the unfamiliar. Such a pattern establishes a clear context for each significant new point and creates natural supportive transitions. The same technique applies to individual sentences. For example, this sequence of sentences follows the familiar-to-unfamiliar pattern:

> Wharton, as the landlord of a building with multiple tenants, has a duty of reasonable care for areas of common use. Wharton's duty with respect to common areas includes the duty to inspect, safeguard, and issue warnings concerning dangerous conditions. Although the first floor foyer by intention and use is a common area, the plywood door is less certainly one, and the dangerous renovation area is probably not for common use. Therefore, social guest Revere's belief that the renovation area was a common area is neither decisive nor reasonable.

Note the progression in each sentence from established information to significant new material, preparing the reader for the final opinion that Revere's belief is unreasonable:

Known material	New information
Wharton as the landlord . . .	has a duty of care for common areas
the duty includes . . .	to issue warnings concerning dangerous conditions
the first floor foyer is a common area . . .	the renovation area is not for common use
therefore, social guest Revere's belief that it was a common area . . .	is neither decisive nor reasonable

This given/new sequence not only permits you to better control reader response, it also makes it clear that the writer is organized on every level of the document—from the overall structure to the individual sentence.

Parallel Structure

Parallelism—the use of the same grammatical structures—is another technique that applies to large-scale organization (see Chapter 3) but is key to individual sentence strategies as well. When attorneys sit down to write, they are faced with more information than fits comfortably in short sentences. So they tend to write long ones. The longer the sentence, the more important it is to keep the components parallel so the reader doesn't get lost in your prose's shifting directions. For example, this sentence contains a lot of information presented in a topsy turvy fashion:

> Would the defendant's frequent communications with Rayman that she gave specific directions to hire and to fire, the fact that she sequenced the renovation work, and the materials used allow a jury to conclude that Nelson Rayman was merely her employee?

When placed in parallel order and structure, the sentence reads so much more clearly:

> Would the defendant's frequent communicating with Rayman, her specific directing to hire and fire, her sequencing of the renovations, and her providing the work materials allow a jury to conclude that Nelson Rayman was merely her employee?

Even short sentences gain added forcefulness when they are parallel. This sentence, for instance: "No warning notices were posted, and adequate precautions were omitted by the defendant," becomes much stronger when written in the active voice and in parallel structure: "The defendant posted no warning notices and took inadequate precautions." It's hard to miss the writer's point in that sentence.

Once you're able to recognize the major problems lawyers have in composing sentences, you can edit specifically for those problems. As in any task, the job gets easier the more you practice the technique. But no matter how talented you are as an attorney or as a writer, revising legal prose is a painstaking task requiring patience and a good set of tools. The following quick reference list reviews the main tools necessary for editing at the sentence level.

CHECKLIST: EDITING SENTENCES

1.   Find all passive verbs. Can you switch them to the more dynamic active voice?

2.   Take a close look at each form of the verb *to be*. Have you missed an opportunity to use a more vivid verb?

3.   Do any of your nouns contain the seeds of a verb? If so, change them to their verb forms to make your prose more lively and persuasive.

4.   If you write more than two "who," "which," or "that" clauses or more than three prepositional phrases in a row, reduce these overweight constructions.

5.   Evaluate your paragraphs for sentence variety. Effective, readable prose varies sentence lengths, beginnings, and types.

6.   Make sure you begin sentences with established material and end with new or emphatic information—and use parallel structure.

Problem Solution

1.   To overcome the "employee/independent contractor" legal status vested on the Wharton-Rayman contract, Revere must prove that Wharton controlled the work details' mode and method, thus changing their contractual relationship to give Wharton "right of control."

Main problems corrected:

Overuse of prepositional phrases, too many "to be" verbs

2.   Wharton is vicariously liable if Rayman's inherently dangerous work or his lack of proper precautions created a nondelegable duty of care.

Main problem corrected:

Passive voice

3.   Assuming the Courts decide as a matter of law that Jan Wharton hired Nelson Rayman as an independent contractor, we must prove Rayman's renovation work inherently dangerous, making Wharton liable for any negligence.

Main problems corrected:

Passive voice, clause and phrase strings

4.   Although the courts liberally define *employee* as a matter of public policy, without statutory authority, they must turn to common law tort applications to determine how the act defines *employee*. (This sentence makes little sense. The original exemplifies tangled prose reflecting tangled thinking.)

Main problems corrected:

Nounisms, prepositional phrase strings, passive voice

Chapter 6

Writing as an Advocate—Persuasive Strategies

Problem

Read these excerpts from summary judgment briefs. Notice in particular the persuasive techniques each writer employs to advocate the client's position. When you consider how the rhetorical elements of audience, purpose, and tone apply in each passage, do you detect flaws in the writers' approaches to advocacy? Are there other problems you see that undercut the effectiveness of these writers as advocates?

1.   Should a prospective tenant who has been invited by an owner to inspect the premises be found at summary judgment to be a mere licensee or trespasser?

2.   Persevering in his search for an apartment despite defendant's failure to light the premises, William Revere fell into a gaping chasm and sustained such debilitating injuries that he has suffered constant, excruciating pain since that moment.

3.   Is an employee an independent contractor when his employer controls materials, directs laborers, alters work methods, and generally involves herself in the process of the renovation?

4.   Must summary judgment be denied when there are genuine disputes as to whether Wharton's invitation to "look around" coupled with the appearance of the premises permits the inference that Revere was an invitee?

The problem solution appears at the end of the chapter.

This chapter focuses on persuasive techniques lawyers can use to write convincing arguments. At this point in the legal writing process, you've completed all the research, explored various alternatives for your client, and are ready to argue for the most favorable solution. How can you use language to drive your point home persuasively, but *fairly*? As much of the material in the previous chapters has suggested, effective persuasion is a matter of tone and therefore dependent on the psychology you use to connect with your reader. Advocacy delicately balances audience, purpose, and tone, creating exactly the right language to make your point. If you tip the balance, the entire argument may fall apart.

OBJECTIVE VERSUS PERSUASIVE PROSE

Many people believe the stereotype that all lawyers have forked tongues—they manipulate words to suit their own ends and never tell the straight story. Part of the reason for this impression is that some attorneys don't recognize the difference between objective and subjective prose, nor do they understand when each is appropriate and why. Novice legal writers, especially, have difficulty avoiding the urge to use dramatic language when they argue opinions, not realizing that effective persuasion stems from a logical base, not an emotional one. Good lawyers control language to present their clients in the best possible light, and good persuasive writing gains the audience's trust by presenting both sides of an argument. Writing as an advocate means knowing how to argue your client's position strongly while sounding objective. That means *you* have to be objective first in order to determine how to present the client's case persuasively without resorting to propaganda or other fact-twisting techniques.

Audience Reconsidered

The best test for knowing when to be objective is to once again consider the audience. Obviously, interoffice memoranda must be objective because the audience is made up of colleagues working together to determine the best legal recourse for the client. Client letters and the various forms of interrogatory writing are more objective than persuasive because the writer's primary purpose is not to convince, but to disseminate or gather information. But when you write a brief for the Court, you are definitely arguing an opinion and can benefit from reaching the audience's emotions as well as intellect.

Speaking to those emotions opens Pandora's box for many legal writers as they tip immediately into propaganda and undermine the soundness of their arguments. Simply because you need to convince your audience of your opinion does not give you license to bend the truth. That's a lesson many attorneys haven't learned—hence the stereotype of the lawyer with the forked tongue.

The Limits of Emotional Appeal

For many writers, prose is either totally objective, or it is totally subjective, aimed directly at the audience's emotions. When attorneys write as advocates, they sometimes are tempted to write melodrama rather than clear argument. They load the language with sanguine appeals rather than with empirical logic. As an example, this passage illustrates what happens when a legal writer inserts his own judgments into the memo and assumes the reader will buy this slanted view:

> A practical matter that might make the Court hesitant to find for Casterbank is the problem of distinguishing and proving embarrassment, humiliation, and other nondisabling mental injuries within the head of a woman diagnosed by her own doctors as an obsessive compulsive neurotic schizophrenic with a well-developed obsessional component and reactive depression secondary to job loss. Read that "certified nut." A judge may well cringe in his robe at the thought of the potential parade of frauds and Freuds in his courtroom, especially given the defendant's connections in the health care field.

There are two problems here. First, the writer has confused biased language with logical argument; and second, although exaggerated language may sometimes work in oral advocacy, it rarely works in written form. When a person speaks in front of an audience, the entire physical personality comes into play: the voice inflections, the facial expressions, the gestures, and so forth. But in writing, the words on the page are the only visible indicators of emotion. Whereas the courtroom lawyer's clever language may fit the natural drama inherent in speaking before a jury, the physical elements of drama are not available on the page. For most readers, consciously emotive writing seems phony.

Think of it this way: When you watch a movie or a play, you respond to the actors' interpretations of the lines. The speeches come alive as you get caught up in the way the actors deliver the lines, not in the words themselves. But if you were to read those same speeches as they appear in the written script, they probably would seem overly dramatic. Few sensible people could repress a smirk if they read, "Of all the cities and all the gin joints in the world, and you walked into mine?" But when Bogart says almost the same words to Bergman, most of us accept the emotion as appropriate. The same holds true for the preceding legal example. Try reading it aloud as if you were arguing in front of a jury. You can make those words effective by using all the tricks of a good actor. But on the written page, the lines seem overbearing.

It's also true that when readers become aware you are intentionally appealing to emotion, they will wonder why you need to do it. Can't your argument stand on its logic? In cases where your emotional prose either replaces logic or overshadows it, you've reached the limits of emotional appeal. Keep in mind that these limits are easy to reach. It's usually better to keep your dramatic language in check rather than giving it free rein. The following examples of legal prose heavily laden with emotion should illustrate the need to maintain a better balance:

> 1. Casterbank's refusal to assist occurred within a highly charged work arena: the realm of a medical institution. Are there not significant reasons for making a distinction between employee-employer relations and behavior within a medical context and those relations outside this environment? Medical contexts, including the South End Clinic, are places in which life-threatening operations, including minors' abortions, occur on a daily basis. Within this realm, is it not possible that particular and perhaps higher standards of obedience and attention to rules and regulations, both internal and statutory, should apply?
> 2. Jan Wharton hired Nelson Rayman, an engineer and independent contractor, to renovate One Traverso Street. This was Rayman's first project involving the renovation of an entire building, but Wharton voiced her confidence in his ability by describing him as a strange but creative personality.
> 3. On the particularly dark July night, Billy Revere, the plaintiff, wandered into the first floor renovation area at One Traverso Street. Noticing that the temporary plywood door was open six inches, he pushed open the door despite it being dark inside. After stumbling around looking for a light switch, Billy reached what he knew to be a stud wall and passed through it. After a couple of steps, he fell into the open hole.

These examples illustrate the writers' attempts to portray the factual situation as extraordinary (example 1), to undercut the defendant's character and ability (example 2), and to connote the stupidity of the plaintiff's actions (example 3). Unfortunately, the extreme use of emotion undermines the writer's intent in each paragraph.

FAIR USE OF CONNOTATIVE LANGUAGE

When is it appropriate to use emotional language, and how do you indicate emotion in a subtle fashion? These questions don't have absolute answers, but a good starting point is to explore how emotionally loaded prose can backfire.

Slanted Language as Detrimental

Your primary job as an advocate is to gain the reader's trust in your point of view. If you've researched the case well and have at your command logically organized support for your position, you can present that position without apology. The audience should trust the soundness of the argument—but you must indicate your trust in the audience. That's key. If your argument is well reasoned, intelligent readers will see the logic. But if you rely on slanted emotional language, chances are readers will realize the ploy and decide either you don't trust their intelligence or your argument is more propaganda than logic. Either realization is fatal to your purpose as an advocate.

Try this test yourself. Read the following sentence from a legal memorandum, and monitor your reactions:

> In countering Vivian Casterbank's allegations, the clinic needs to establish that the recent appellate court decisions do not carve out a niche for Casterbank to slither into.

How do you feel about the soundness of this statement? Do you naturally rise to Casterbank's defense? When confronted with such obviously slanted language, most readers feel the need to argue the opposite side of the issue simply because they sense the writer is being unfair. Obviously, this example exaggerates the point, but it comes from the first draft of an office memorandum written by a serious young law student. Later versions temper the emotions. Try the test once more with this excerpt from a brief:

> Should it be fair that a person dedicated to solving the problems of adequate low income housing be held liable when a trespasser trips and falls in a building owned by a person with a social conscience?

As both of these examples illustrate, legal writers should realize that biased language usually backfires. Make sure you indicate your respect for the audience's intelligence as readers and as decision makers; in turn, they will respond with greater respect for your position.

The Traps of Fallacious Logic

When attorneys become immersed in a case, it's easy for them to lose sight of objectivity and not realize how biased they really are. In these instances, legal writers trying to structure a logical argument may fall into the trap of fallacious logic. Although these fallacies may sound perfectly logical to the writer who is living and breathing the case, the faulty thinking behind them is usually apparent to the readers. A list of some of these pitfalls should serve as warning.

1.   *Generalizing from a particular:* The writer assumes that what is true in one instance is true always.

Example:
Nelson Rayman employed a worker who smoked marijuana. Therefore, it stands to reason that many of his employees smoke pot.

2.   *Overinclusive premise:* The writer places everything under one label.

Example:
Everyone who has been under psychiatric care is unable to make mentally sound decisions. Vivian Casterbank's suit against the clinic proceeds from her mental instability.

3.   *Guilt by association:* The writer suggests that a person or an organization behaves the same way as others in the same circumstances.

Example:
The South End Family Planning Clinic is probably a back alley operation making quick bucks from the plight of unwed teenagers.

4.   *Begging the question:* The writer assumes a premise the reader may question. (This is especially dangerous in issue statements.)

Example:
Even if Rayman were an independent contractor, could a jury still infer that the defendant's failure to post warning notices at One Traverso Street made her vicariously liable because she had a nondelegable duty of care to take such precautions? (The writer assumes the duty of care is nondelegable.)

5.   *Evading the issue:* The writer beats around the proverbial bush, but does it with style.

Example:
What is the relationship between the owner-renovator of a building being turned into half residential and half commercial space and his general contractor when the owner-renovator drafts plans with the general contractor but lets the contractor buy the tools and hire the workers but later intervenes to fire a worker who was smoking marijuana?

6.   *Nonsequitur* (Latin for "it does not follow"): The writer does not proceed logically; the connections between the sentences or the ideas aren't clear.

Example:
Although the Michigan Worker's Compensation Act makes benefits under the act exclusive, in the Michigan Appeals Court, common law exception to exclusivity was allowed. (This sentence suggests that the appellate court is lawless.)

7.   *Sequence as cause:* The writer assumes a chronological chain of events, each event causing the one that follows. Many

superstitions are based on this faulty logic—walking under a ladder causes any subsequent bad luck, for instance.

Example:
Because Casterbank was placed under psychiatric care after the clinic fired her, her mental disability resulted from the wrongful discharge and is actionable under the MWCA.

8. *Argument ad hominem* (Latin for "argument at the person"): This simply means the writer can't find a logical leg to stand on, so he or she begins name-calling or using other tactics directed at the opponent's character. (If you can reduce your opponent to this tactic, you have probably won the battle of logic.)

Example:
No reasonable jury could find in favor of Jan Wharton, an unscrupulous slumlord whose dereliction of duty is expected of someone of her caliber.

9. *Analogy as fact:* This faulty logic especially plagues lawyers because they spend so much time analogizing cases. The flaw in the argument occurs when the writer assumes what is true for the analogous case will definitely apply to the case at hand.

Example:
Based on *Slayton v. Michigan Host, Inc.*, a case in which a waitress was fired for refusing to wear a sexually revealing uniform, Casterbank can argue that her discharge is also discriminatory, and the clinic deliberately disregarded her fundamental rights as an employee. (But the applicability of *Slayton* turns on whether Casterbank's discharge is analogous to discrimination based on sex.)

As you can see, the trap in all these examples springs shut when the writer makes assumptions without first establishing grounds to do so. Lawyers are well trained to provide adequate support for their arguments, but they sometimes fall victim to prefabricated thought patterns that result in false assumptions. If you're aware of that possible danger, you may be able to avoid it—forewarned is forearmed.

Subtle Persuasion

Given these cautions about the dangers of slanted language and fallacious logic, how can the legal writer use language to persuade fairly? Now that you know what *not* to do, you should determine what makes advocacy effective.

First, put yourself in the reader's place. If you read an argument that strikes you as one-sided, you're naturally going to mistrust it. But if all the facts and all sides are clearly represented—even if one side is advocated—you're more likely to buy the argument because you feel the writer has nothing to hide. Second, check the balance between persuasive words and straightforward logic. Heavy-handed persuasion signals weak logic that needs ballast to be convincing. As a writer, you should acknowledge the reader's talent for knowing when you're shoveling the manipulative diction instead of allowing the argument's own merits to do the convincing. In almost every instance, it's clear when the writer lacks confidence in the material because the argument seems rigged and the persuasive techniques paramount.

The following two passages present the same set of facts from *Revere v. Wharton.* In each instance, the writer tells the truth without "doctoring" the facts, but the language preconditions the reader's response. Note the skillful—not imposing—use of language with emotional overtones:

1. While looking for available apartments, pursuant to the landlord's express invitation, Mr. Revere went through an open door at the rear of the first floor common foyer, which, he believed, led to common passageways and other available apartments. Unknown to him, there was a large unguarded and unlighted hole in the floor near the open door that was created during ongoing renovations. Mr. Revere took several cautious steps in search of a light switch. Immediately beyond a partially finished wall, Mr. Revere fell into an unguarded hole, sustaining disabling leg injuries.

2. At the rear of the foyer, an unfinished plywood door normally kept padlocked by the contractor during nonworking hours led to the first floor space that was still under renovation for commercial use. On the night of the plaintiff's accident, he left the second floor party and—without the knowledge or permission of the defendant or her tenant—groped into an unlighted area beyond the plywood door, allegedly in search of an "available"

apartment. After proceeding several steps in the dark, Revere came to an unfinished stud wall through which he stepped. After a few more steps into the darkness, Revere fell into an unguarded opening in the floor created by defendant Nelson Rayman, the contractor who was renovating the first floor area. Revere sustained personal injuries as a result of the fall.

Obviously, word choice plays an immense role in how the audience perceives the situation. In the first version, the plaintiff's account, Revere takes cautious steps to find the light switch, implying a very short distance traveled and a sensible action. In the defendant's version, Revere gropes through obviously unfinished walls and continues unreasonably through the darkness until he falls into the hole. Each writer has taken the facts and chosen to feature different elements more favorable to his or her individual clients. More important, each has chosen words and phrases that create emotional response in the reader. "Grope," for instance, reflects negatively on Revere; "took cautious steps" is a positive statement. In the first passage, it's "Mr." Revere; in the latter, it's simply "Revere." But in neither version are the facts so slanted or the emotions so overbearing that the reader can't understand the actual happenings or make an intelligent decision.

Rather than relying on propaganda or slanted language, the effective writer emphasizes the argument's positive themes by subtly weaving them through the text in convincing designs. Even sentence structure contributes to the subtle persuasiveness here. In the first description, the first sentence begins with phrases that establish a justifiable context for the plaintiff's actions. In other words, "While looking for available apartments, pursuant to the landlord's express invitation" subtly wins the reader's sympathy for the ending actions in the sentence: "Mr. Revere went through an open door." The writer uses the same technique again in the next statement: "Unknown to him" precedes the description of the dangerous hole. By beginning sentences with phrases favorable to the client, the writer leads the audience to view the questionable actions in a favorable light. You can see the same techniques used in the second example as well, but for a different effect: "At the rear of the foyer, an unfinished plywood door normally kept padlocked" introduces the fact that the door was open.

These two paragraphs illustrate how writers can use individual words and sentence structures to persuade the reader. But beyond the techniques applicable to single sentences, legal writers should find opportunities to carry the subtle emotion of themes throughout the prose.

ESTABLISHING KEY THEMES

When your goal as a writer is to persuade the reader, the most effective method is to research the problem thoroughly and present convincing legal support for the argument. To do that, you can subtly influence the audience by emphasizing certain themes within the argument. Think of your prose as a musical composition in which several key melodic lines repeat, creating an emotional response in the listener. The more complicated the composition, the more the composer depends on the repeating themes to tie the piece together. As lawyers rather than composers, your first job is to define the themes and differentiate them from other parts of the argument.

The Difference Between Thesis and Theme

Particularly when writing the legal brief, you need to pay attention to threading key advocacy themes throughout the argument. The first step is to understand the relationship between thesis and theme. The *thesis* is the main point you're trying to argue. For instance, the thesis of a summary judgment brief on *Revere* v. *Wharton* might be phrased this way:

> By her Motion for Summary Judgment, defendant Wharton seeks to ignore the substantial disputes concerning the boundaries of the common areas, the extent of her duty, the reasonableness of her precautions, and her degree of knowledge of dangerous conditions. Given these disputes which are traditionally jury issues, defendant's Motion for Summary Judgment should be denied.

Note how directly the writer states this main point.

The *theme* is a motif established by orchestrated connotative language reinforcing the thesis. The theme differs from the thesis in that it relies on inference and suggested meaning rather than direct statement. In one argument there can be several key themes running throughout. For example, part of the preceding thesis that can be thematically supported is Wharton's knowledge of the dangerous conditions. This paragraph establishes the thematic motif by repeating words that reinforce her prior knowledge of the dangers. Any reference to danger or her knowledge continues the theme:

> Ms. Wharton *had known* for several weeks that *rotten floor boards* would soon be removed from the renovation area. She *also knew* that the renovation area was *unlighted* and that *no warnings* were posted. Defendant landlord *knew* the renovation area was potentially *dangerous* to *unsuspecting* visitors such as Revere in that she had arranged for the plywood door to be *secured* with a lock. Nonetheless, Ms. Wharton did nothing to *warn* Mr. Revere or other party-goers about the *dangerous* ongoing renovations. Instead, she extended an open invitation to Revere and others to "look around" in the *foreseeably dangerous* building.

Using Equivalence Chains

As illustrated by the paragraph in the last example of theme, writers can repeat thesis words or their synonyms to create a pattern that emphasizes the particular point. These equivalence chains of meaning can help both to reinforce the main idea and to make the argument cohere. In so doing, they serve as implicit transitions that hold the argument together. If you consciously attempt to use such patterns, you are more likely to stick to the main point and proceed logically. As in other writing techniques requiring subtlety, the danger is that novice writers may sometimes go overboard and use the same word excessively. For example, the following argument obviously attempts to emphasize the fact that the renovation area was openly accessible to Revere:

> The *open* invitation to use the foyer doorway, implicit in Wharton's design, was reinforced by the door itself being *open*. In both *Argo* and *Portee*, an *open* door was pivotal to finding an implied invitation. In *Argo*, a business invitee case, a blind door-to-door salesman fell into an *open hole* immediately beyond an *unlocked* door. The court noted: "Indeed by leaving the door *open* within *easy access* of the sidewalk, the possessor had issued the sales-

man an implicit invitation" 438 Pa. 265 A. 2d 786. Similarly, in *Portee*, authorities had removed the basement door during a prior raid on the basement speakeasy. The landlord did not replace the door, and the guest of a speakeasy patron was justified in traversing the *open doorway*. Like the plaintiffs in *Argo* and *Portee*, Mr. Revere was justified in relying on the *open door* as an *open invitation*. Revere's reliance was especially reasonable because other doors in the building had been purposefully left *open* by Wharton to facilitate prospective tenants' viewing of available apartments. This implies that *open* areas are *open* for inspection.

Although the argument in the previous paragraph is sound, the overuse of the word *open* becomes an irritant to the reader and ultimately works against the writer rather than for her. To best establish themes in legal prose, you should determine in advance what parts of the thesis can be supported thematically and then make a list of synonyms for each thematic idea. For example, in *Revere* v. *Wharton*, several themes might work for effective advocacy, depending on the legal issue you're arguing. Think of as many words as possible to emphasize the possible themes:

Thesis	Possible themes
Revere exceeded the scope of his invitation.	unreasonable actions obvious renovation area
Wharton is not vicariously liable to Revere.	Rayman's independence and control over the project Wharton's lack of knowledge of the dangerous hole

In the first draft, take a minute to underline your connotative words and check to see if you're overdoing it. Remember, the whole idea of advocacy is to influence the audience without seeming to try. For instance, if your thesis is Wharton's lack of knowledge about the dangers, don't go so far as to make her seem idiotic, and if you're arguing against Revere on the status issue, don't go to the extreme of portraying him as nothing more than a drunk. Once the readers become aware of your attempts to manipulate their thinking, your battle becomes twice as hard to win. If overdone, persuasive language can turn from a strength into a weakness.

ANTICIPATING THE OPPONENT

Another key to arguing effectively is to include the opponent's view. By so doing, you anticipate the counterarguments and can go a long way toward defusing them before they're actually made. One word of caution: even though you should include the opponent's argument, don't spend the majority of your time rebutting it or degrading it. To do so is to feature that view instead of your own. But there are some strategies for dealing with the opposing view that will strengthen your own stance without degrading the other point of view.

Including the Opposing View

Many writing experts suggest that including the opponent's view within your argument effectively balances your opinion and takes care of your duty to recognize the other side. Of course, you must include the opposing argument to avoid presenting half of the story—a propaganda technique that usually backfires. But merely paying lip service to the other side does no service to your view and probably appears little more than dutiful. You must use the counterargument effectively to enhance your own position.

How do you do this? A two-part technique answers this question. First, order the material to place your argument in the stronger position. Although some rhetoricians will tell you to put your point *last* because the final spot has greater impact, that technique means you're always featuring the opponent's argument by putting it first. The best compromise to this problem is to begin a discussion on a legal issue by (1) stating concisely your view of the problem, (2) *briefly* giving the opposite argument, and (3) expanding on your view in the final position. By so doing, you allow your argument to surround the counterview, literally fencing it in. It also gives you the final word. This position allows you to refer to the preceding view, giving you the leverage of comparison; and it also places your opinion last, making it the final idea the reader carries away from the discussion.

Second, when you include the counterargument, write it in clear, direct language. When you phrase it, ask yourself whether the attorney for the other side would agree that your statement is fair. Forcing yourself to state the opposing viewpoint in an unbiased manner allows you to really understand that view. If you're going to argue against something, it's essential that you understand it. It's surprising how many attorneys never actually consider the other argument's merits in their urgency to do battle. The best lawyers realize that legal practice isn't about winning and losing so much as it is concerned with solving problems. To resolve a conflict, you must understand all of its parts. For example, the following passage doesn't present both sides of the problem and therefore isn't nearly as persuasive as the revised version that follows it:

First version:
Wharton had actual knowledge of the open and dangerous hole, but failed in her clear duty to safeguard them or to issue proper warnings. Not only did she fail to warn her unsuspecting guests, she actually uttered a misleading open invitation to the disaster that befell Mr. Revere.

This paragraph is one-sided and certainly seems slanted toward defendant Revere's position. If the lawyer revises the argument to begin with Wharton's view and then logically explains why that view is unreasonable, the prose will be more trustworthy and more persuasive. In the following version, note how concisely the opposing argument is stated—the writer wastes little time discussing it:

Second version:
Defendant Wharton should not win summary judgment on the basis that she did not know about the dangers at the construction site. A major thesis of Wharton's motion for summary judgment is that she lacked actual knowledge of the open foyer door and dangerous hole in the renovation area. However, Wharton knew of the extensive damage to the floor, and she knew for several weeks that Rayman planned to remove the rotten floorboards in the renovation area near the foyer. A jury might reasonably infer that Wharton thereby had actual knowledge of the hole. Once she had actual knowledge of the defects, she had a clear duty to safeguard them or to issue proper warnings, both of which she failed to do.
Even if Wharton did not have actual knowledge of the open door and dangerous hole, a jury could find that she had sufficient time during her three hours at the premises to fulfill her duty to inspect and safeguard common areas, especially in light of the

known renovations and anticipated floor repairs. Similarly, a jury could find that Wharton failed in her duty to warn unsuspecting guests such as Revere about the dangerous ongoing renovations on the first floor. Not only did she fail to warn, she actually uttered a misleading open invitation to disaster.

By clearly stating your opinion, then the opponent's, and placing your argument in the stronger final position, you gain more control over the reader's intellectual and emotional view of the problem. And because you have given a fair version of the opponent's argument, you have probably also gained the reader's trust. You seem confident and logical—both essential ingredients for a persuasive appeal.

Undercutting the Opposition

By including the counterargument, you have set the stage for explaining why your view is more sound. It's important to realize that your job is to strongly express your logical stance, not to waste time tearing down the opposition. Effective arguing keeps the focus on your view, not the opponent's. No argument will appear persuasive if the attorney spends more time leveling attacks on the other side than she does constructing a solid logical framework for her own side. Check your primary focus to make sure you include the opposition, but that you don't make it the center of attention. If it is central, then you probably are doing a good public relations job for the opposing attorney. Remember, your argument—not the opponent's—needs the reader's attention.

Take a minute or so at this point to review the suggestions for effective persuasion presented in this chapter. The following summary of the main points should help you turn the advice given here into techniques you can apply to your own work.

CHECKLIST: WRITING AS AN ADVOCATE

1.   *Base your argument on logic, not emotion.* Use subjective language to enhance your appeal to the audience's intellect, not to replace it.

2.   *Respect the audience as readers and decision makers.* Provide enough information to allow them to make decisions; don't decide for them by determining what information they should and should not have.

3.   *Put yourself in the audience's place.* Do you feel unfairly manipulated? Use techniques you would feel comfortable with if you were on the receiving end of the legal documents.

4.   *Avoid fallacious logic by providing ample support for all assertions.* Never make assumptions without proving their validity.

5.   *Check the balance between persuasive words and straightforward logic.* If the persuasive language outweighs the logic, rethink the argument and revise the prose.

6.   *Establish key themes to reinforce the thesis by creating image patterns and equivalence chains.* These subtle forms of persuasion depend on your orchestration of connotative meaning.

7.   *Order the argument so that your opinion comes first.* Then include the opposing viewpoint in a concise, direct manner. Expand on your argument in the stronger final position.

8.   *Focus primarily on your view, not the opponent's.* Don't spend the majority of the argument refuting the other side instead of asserting your own opinion.

9.   *Don't be defensive.* You must argue your client's position persuasively, but you must sound confidently objective.

Problem Solution

1.   The slanted language ("mere licensee or trespasser") colors the reader's response, and the statement unjustly asserts that the owner invited the prospective tenant to inspect the dangerous renovation area. This begs the question of whether the renovation site is a common area.

2.   The overly emotional language backfires here. The subjective language so far outweighs the logic of the argument that most intelligent readers will feel manipulated and patronized.

3.   By using the words *employee* and *employer*, the writer has decided for the reader that the contractor is not

independent. Further, the rest of the statement falsely assumes that the defendant controlled the work methods. This has yet to be proven.

4.   This writer begins negatively, thereby causing the audience to start from the assumption that summary judgment should be denied. It's an uphill battle then to convince the reader otherwise, once the negative impression has been created. It would be much better to say: "Because Wharton expressly invited the guests to 'look around,' and because the whole building was undergoing renovation, could a jury reasonably infer that Revere was an invitee as a matter of law?"

Chapter 7

Moving from Office Memorandum to Trial Brief

Generally, a document for the purpose of analyzing a legal problem is a legal memorandum. When the purpose is to persuade, the document is a legal brief. Of course, reducing all legal documents to two major categories is as artificial as dividing everything absolutely into black or white, neglecting the gray areas. Within the memorandum category, for instance, can appear the office memo as well as the memorandum to the court, and within the other category are the trial brief and the appellate brief. To illustrate the different writing strategies necessary for analyzing and for persuading, this chapter concentrates only on the office memorandum and the trial brief as representative documents. Each exemplifies the specific techniques needed for the two kinds of legal writing. Although they resemble each other in important ways, the memorandum and the brief differ in audience, purpose, and tone. This chapter compares the two, noting the similarities and differences and applying the techniques discussed in the previous six chapters.

THE LEGAL OFFICE MEMORANDUM

As suggested earlier in this book, the office memo's main function is to discuss possible solutions to a client's problem. Your audience for such a document is your colleagues who read it primarily for information. To meet their needs, you should resist the temptation to write as an advocate and should maintain an objective tone. If you are writing a legal memorandum, this advice doesn't prevent you from taking a stand and analyzing the merits of one solution over another. But it does mean that you should do so in the spirit of discussion, not persuasion. Present the alternatives, and then explain which one will most likely benefit the client. Keep in mind that *the legal memorandum is an exploratory document.* It should define the problem (issue) and explore the possible solutions.

Once you've decided on a plan of action, you shift audiences from your colleagues to the courts, and you change your purpose from discussing possibilities to advocating a solution— you move from memorandum to brief.

THE TRIAL BRIEF

The legal brief presents the attorney's opinions to the world outside of the law office. As a document, its primary function is to persuade the Court to take a particular view of the legal problem and act accordingly. In order to convince the Court, the writer should adopt a persuasive tone that not only appeals to logic, but also appeals to emotion. *Unlike the memorandum, the brief doesn't explore possible alternatives; it directly advocates one solution.*

Legal briefs come in two types: the appellate brief and the trial brief. The appellate brief, as its name suggests, addresses the appeals court to defend or challenge a lower court's decision. Because the appeals court is primarily concerned with establishing new precedents applicable to many situations, the appellate brief is necessarily more formal. Its point headings deal with policy and general rules of law rather than specific facts of the case at hand. Trial briefs support or oppose various motions before the original trial court, focusing directly on the specific case. This type of brief is sometimes called a "memorandum to the court," but it is not an office memo. The trial brief is used here to highlight the basic differences between legal memoranda and legal briefs.

SAMPLE OFFICE MEMORANDUM AND TRIAL BRIEF COMPARED

The following pages compare, section by section, an office memorandum and a trial brief. It's important to note that the order of material differs between the memorandum and the legal brief. For comparison's sake, similar sections are presented together below, but you should be aware of the following preferred order for the major sections:

Memorandum	Brief
1. Issue statement	1. Questions presented
2. Summary	2. Facts

3. Facts   3. Summary of argument
4. Legal analysis 4. Argument
5. Conclusion   5. Conclusion

Similar sections from each document appear together below, their proximity emphasizing the differing techniques. After each comparison is a short comment on the primary differences.

Memorandum

TO: *Revere* v. *Wharton* File
FROM: Supervisor
RE: Wharton's liability to Revere for negligence in common
        areas
DATE: January 16, 1985

Issue:

(1) Under the 1974 Tenement Building and Multiple Premises Act, is Wharton, the landlord of One Traverso Street, liable to Revere, a tenant's social guest, for personal injuries resulting from Wharton's failure to inspect, safeguard, or issue warnings concerning the open door, the renovations, and the dangerous hole in or accessible from first floor common areas?
(2) Is the Court likely to decide issues of common area liability as a matter of law at summary judgment, or are there disputed facts or law/fact issues making summary judgment inappropriate?

Brief

COMMONWEALTH OF PENNSYLVANIA

COUNTY, §.   SUPERIOR COURT
                             NO. 98765

WILLIAM REVERE, Plaintiff)	PLAINTIFF'S MEMORANDUM IN OPPOSITION TO WHARTON'S FIRST MOTION FOR SUMMARY JUDGMENT ON COUNT II
)) VS.)) JAN WHARTON, *ET AL.*,) Defendants)	

Plaintiff, William Revere, submits this memorandum in opposition to defendant Wharton's first motion for summary judgment on count II of the complaint.

Questions presented:

1. Could a jury conclude that the defendant landlord gave William Revere reason to believe that the open doorway leading off of the first floor common foyer led to common areas available for his use as a prospective tenant and a tenant's lawful guest?
2. May defendant landlord be liable to William Revere for negligently permitting his foreseeable access from the first floor common foyer to the dangerous renovation area immediately beyond the open door?
3. Could a jury conclude that defendant landlord breached her duty to inspect the common foyer and the accessible renovation area during her three-hour attendance at a tenant's party or that she breached her duty to issue proper warnings to unsuspecting guests concerning the known ongoing dangerous renovations?
4. Could a jury conclude that defendant landlord had sufficient notice of the dangerous hole and sufficient opportunity to observe the open door to be charged with actual knowledge of these dangerous conditions?

Comment

Of special note here is the memorandum's lack of emotional overtones. In the "questions presented," the writer presents the legal questions in a straightforward fashion, with no attempt to color the reader's response. The trial brief, however, definitely leads the reader to a predetermined conclusion. By the phrasing of each question, the attorney has indicated the conclusions he advocates; whether a jury "could conclude that . . ." leads the reader to the appropriate response of "yes, a jury may conclude. . . ." Even the wording of the brief's questions connote the writer's opinion: "foreseeable access," "dangerous renovation area," "unsuspecting guests," and so forth.

Contributing to the persuasive effect is the order in which the questions appear. They provide a step-by-step structure confirming Revere's victimhood. First, Wharton gave Revere reason to believe the open doorway led to common areas. Second, she was negligent in not seeing that the door was open. Third, she didn't warn the guests about the dangerous renovations. Fourth, she failed to inspect the premises and safeguard them, even though she had sufficient time to do so. In the phrasing and the ordering of these questions, the writer has carefully focused the lens through which the reader views the case, providing all information, but placing favorable points in the foreground.

Memorandum

Facts:

While attending a party on July 20, 1984, William Revere fell into an unguarded hole in a separate renovation area of a building owned by Jan Wharton. Revere has sued Wharton, alleging in part that she failed in her duty to safeguard the common areas.

On July 20, 1984, Jan Wharton, the owner and landlord of One Traverso Street, had three occupied residential households in a building undergoing further residential and commercial renovation. That evening both Wharton and William Revere, a tenant's social guest, attended a party on the second floor of One Traverso Street. During the party, Revere overheard Wharton say to several party-goers that three apartments would soon be available, and the guests should "feel free to look around."

Located directly inside the street entrance, the first floor foyer was open for and used for buzzer-controlled access to the second and third floors, which were the residential areas of the building. A normally locked plywood door at the right rear of the foyer was left ajar the night of the party. Beyond the plywood door was the commercial renovation area, including a dangerous, unguarded hole in the floor. The unlighted renovation area had stud walls and was clearly undergoing construction.

Wharton posted no warnings concerning the renovation area and allegedly failed to inspect the area or the open plywood door the night of the party. She denies direct knowledge of the existence of the hole. However, she had generally prevented tenants from using the renovation area, with one exception for a tenant moving a piano.

While allegedly looking for an apartment, Revere passed through the open foyer doorway into the darkened renovation area. Searching for a light switch, Revere passed through the stud wall and fell into the unguarded hole, sustaining serious personal injury.

Brief

Facts:

On the evening of July 20, 1984, William Revere suffered serious personal injury from a fall into a dark unguarded hole in the first floor of One Traverso Street, an occupied multiple tenant unit apartment building owned and operated by defendant Jan Wharton. (Plaintiff's Answers to Defendant Jan Wharton's Answers to Plaintiff's First Set of Interrogatories [R.A.] 11, 16, 18; Defendant Wharton's Answers to Plaintiff's First Set of Interrogatories [W.A.] 2, 50.) Mr. Revere was at One Traverso Street both to attend a housewarming party at a second floor tenant's apartment and to look at newly renovated apartments for rent. [R.A. 10.] While looking for available apartments, following the landlord's express invitation, Mr. Revere went through an open door at the rear of the first floor common foyer, which, he believed, led to common passageways and other available apartments. Unknown to him, near the open door was a large, unguarded, and unlighted hole created during ongoing renovations. [R.A. 11.] Mr. Revere took several cautious steps in search of a light switch. [R.A. 11.] Immediately beyond a partially finished wall, Mr. Revere fell into the unguarded hole and sustained disabling leg injuries. [R.A. 11, 18.]

Mr. Revere and other guests at the party were given permission by defendant landlord to "look around" at the recently renovated apartments. [R.A. 11, 16; W.A. 55.] Although the landlord left three apartment doors open to permit guests to inspect available apartments and although she knew that many guests were familiar with the building, she did not inspect the common areas of the building for dangerous conditions during her three-hour stay at the party. [W.A. 64, 65, 61, 48.] Specifically, the defendant did not check the first floor foyer to make sure that the dangerous renovation area was properly sealed off by a locked door. [W.A. 48.]

Wharton had known for several weeks that rotten floorboards would soon be removed from the renovation area. [W.A. 44, 55.] She also knew the renovation area was unlighted, and no warnings were posted. Defendant landlord knew the renovation area was potentially dangerous to unsuspecting visitors such as Revere because she had arranged for the plywood door to be secured with a lock. [W.A. 61, 62.] Nonetheless, Wharton did nothing to warn Mr. Revere or other party-goers about the dangerous ongoing renovations. Instead, she extended an open invitation to Revere and others to "look around" in the foreseeably dangerous building. [W.A. 48, 55.]

Comment

Obviously, the facts section of the memo is again straightforward, placing all the facts in order and giving equal focus to events both favorable and unfavorable to Revere. But the facts section in the brief provides a built-in opportunity to color the reader's perspective on the case. Placing the facts right after the questions presented encourages the reader to use the description as a persuasive reflection on the problems. (In the memorandum, you recall, the facts appear after the summary, not directly after the issue statements.) In this trial brief, the attorney has used connotative language to create both an intellectual and emotional response favorable to his client. The differences between the objective language of the memo and the persuasive wording of the brief are especially clear in the subtle—but effective—changes the writer makes in presenting these facts:

Revere attends a "housewarming" party; he is not merely a tenant's social guest. In the brief, he takes "several cautious steps" in search of a light switch, instead of simply searching for the switch. Rather than passing through a "stud wall," Revere now goes through a "partially finished wall" and falls into the "large, unguarded, and unlighted hole." The connotations of this phrasing indicate Revere's reasonable behavior while he was victimized by Wharton's negligence. The repetition of the verb *know* in the final paragraph of the brief's facts section reinforces Wharton's shirking of her duty. She "had known" about the rotten floorboards, she "knew" the area was unlighted, and she "knew" it was potentially dangerous. This stacking of the verb makes the final two sentences even more dynamic—although she "knew" so much, *nonetheless Wharton did nothing to warn. . . .* Instead, she extended an invitation to disaster.

Memorandum

Summary:

Because Wharton was the landlord of a building with multiple tenants, her duty of reasonable care for areas of common use extended to Revere, either as Wharton's invitee or as a tenant's social guest. Under this duty, Wharton traditionally is obligated to inspect, safeguard, and issue warnings concerning dangerous conditions within common areas. Although the first floor foyer by intention and use is a common area, the plywood door is less certainly one, and the renovation area was probably not for common use even by implication at the time of Revere's injury. Revere's subjective belief that the darkened, stud wall renovation area was common is neither decisive nor in this case reasonable in redefining the implied boundaries of Wharton's common passageways.

Therefore, if Revere's injury must have occurred in a common area for him to recover, Wharton escapes liability precisely because the renovation area was not for common use. However, Wharton might still be liable for negligently permitting access to a dangerous hole or for not adequately defining the common areas and warning of dangerous conditions accessible from those areas. The negligent access theory of liability seems to be an open issue in Pennsylvania.

The Court might grant partial summary judgment to Wharton on common area boundaries and the unavailability of the negligent access theory. If the negligent access theory remains viable, summary judgment concerning Wharton's knowledge of the renovation area's dangers and on her breach of duty is unlikely because juries traditionally decide such questions.

Brief

Summary of argument:

Defendant landlord had a statutory and common law duty, which she breached, to safeguard all of the common areas of One Traverso Street, including the dangerous renovation area readily accessible from the common first floor foyer. By her motion for summary judgment, the defendant seeks to ignore the substantial disputes concerning the boundaries of the common areas, the extent of her duty, the reasonableness of her precautions, and her degree of knowledge about dangerous conditions. Given these disputes traditionally left for juries to decide, the Court should deny defendant's motion for summary judgment.

By her design of the entrance foyer, by the open door leading to the dangerous hole, and by her open-ended oral invitation, defendant landlord gave Mr. Revere reason to believe that the doorway and renovation area were intended for common use. Accordingly, the door and renovation area are common areas requiring special care. Even if the doorway and the renovation area are not common areas, Wharton has a duty to prevent unsuspecting guests such as Revere from having ready access to the dangerous renovation site.

Defendant Wharton had sufficient notice of the open hole and open doorway to infer her actual knowledge. Even without actual knowledge, however, defendant landlord had ample opportunity to inspect and safeguard the foyer and dangerous renovation area during her three hours at the building. At the least, she could have warned Revere and others about the ongoing renovations. Instead, she issued an open invitation to disaster.

Comment

In the memorandum, the summary explains both positive and negative points about the case. The writer expresses all the probabilities, from Revere's unreasonable subjective belief that the renovation area was common, to Wharton's likely winning summary judgment on the issue of common area boundaries. The point of this summary is to present the options and point out the strengths and weaknesses of each.

Note, however, that the summary of argument in the brief begins with the conclusion: "Defendant landlord had a statutory and common law duty, which she breached. . . ." Here the writer doesn't explore; he asserts the conclusion and then explains why it's logical for the Court to hold this view. As suggested in the questions presented, the summary of argument progresses in step-by-step fashion, leaving little room for a reasonable person to disagree with the seemingly airtight logic. And the summary of argument fulfills its other function of setting up reader expectations for the detailed argument's organization: the argument should follow the same order as the summary of argument. In this instance, the writer begins with the statutory duty, opposes the motion for summary judgment, and then proceeds to give grounds for opposing that motion. The language is connotative, using image patterns and repeating words effectively.

Memorandum

Legal analysis:
A. *The 1974 Tenement Building and Multiple Dwelling Premises Act covers Wharton's common area liability to Revere.*

In 1974, Pennsylvania enacted the Tenement Building and Multiple Premises Act 68 Pa. Cons. Stat. Ann. §250.551-250.552 (Purdon). The act, which reads as follows, clarifies and codifies the common law on a landlord's common area liability.

§250.551 Definitions

As used in this article, the following terms shall have the meanings ascribed to them in this section unless the context otherwise indicates:

(1) "Tenement building" any house or building, or portion thereof, which is intended or designed to be occupied or leased for occupation, or actually occupied, as a home or residence for three or more households living in separate apartments, and doing their cooking upon the premises.

(2) "Apartment" a room or suite of two or more rooms, occupied or leased for occupation, or intended or designed to be occupied, as a domicile.

(3) "Multiple dwelling premises" any area occupied by dwelling units, appurtenances thereto, grounds and facilities which dwelling units are intended or designed to be occupied or leased for occupation, or actually occupied, as individual homes or residences for three or more households. "Multiple dwelling premises" shall include, inter alia, mobile home parks.

§250.552 Landlord's Duties

The retention of control of stairways, passages, roadways, and other common facilities of a tenement building or multiple dwelling premises places upon the landlord, or other possessor, the duty of reasonable care for safety in use. This responsibility of the landlord extends not alone to the individual tenant, but also to his family, servants and employees, business visitors, social guests, and the like. Those who enter in the right of the tenant, even though under his mere license, makes a permissible use of the premises for which the common ways and facilities are provided.

The act clearly covers Wharton as the "landlord" of a "tenement building" or of a "multiple dwelling premise" "occupied" as a "residence" by three or more separate households. *Id.* §250.551 (1), (2), (3). Similarly, the act clearly protects Revere, who was the "social guest" of a tenant. *Id.* 250.552. If the renovation area was common, Revere met the "permissible use" of a common area requirement.

Although the act gives a representative list of what may be common areas, the test, as discussed further below, is "retained control." *Id.* Wharton's duty of care for common areas is broadly but indefinitely defined as "the duty of reasonable care for safety in use." *Id.* The exact parameters of Wharton's duty of care must be abstracted from the caselaw.

B. *By intention, the first floor foyer is a common area; by implication, the plywood door is probably a common door, but the renovation is not for common use even by implication.*

Wharton is only liable for the common areas of One Traverso Street, those over which she retains control. 68 Pa. Stat. Ann. §250.552 (Purdon). The act defines the common areas of retained control in two ways, both applicable to Wharton:

- common areas created expressly by lease terms or by a period of actual use, or;

- common areas created by the structure and design of the building or the actions of the landlord.

As discussed below, under the express test, the first floor foyer is a common area. Under the implicit test, the plywood door is probably a common door. However, the renovation area is neither expressly set off for common use, nor is it implicitly set off despite Revere's subjective belief to the contrary.

(1) The express test makes the foyer a common area.

The areas of retained control, the common areas of a building, may be defined by the express terms of an oral or written lease defining the demised premises and therefore the retained areas. Restatement (second) of Torts §360 Comment d (1965). *Portee* v. *Kronzek* 194 Pa. Super. 193, ___, 166 A. 2d 328, 330 (1960). Definition may also arise from a history of common use. For example, in *Williams* v. *Wolf,* 169 Pa. Super. 628, ___, 84 A. 2d 215, 216-217 (1951), patrons of the two retail food stores used a common aisle, and therefore the landlord was responsible for its proper maintenance. Under the express test, the first floor foyer, as a necessary "passageway" to the second and third floors, is a common area for which Wharton is legally responsible.

(2) The implicit test makes the door common.

Where the lease and historical use are less than explicit, the jury may decide what are the implied common areas. For example, in *Portee* there was no evidence that the speakeasy leased the whole basement. Therefore, the jury could find that the basement stairway was impliedly for common use. Similarly, where an outside balcony was the only access to and from a hotel annex, the balcony could be found a necessary common passageway. *Parsons* v. *Drake* 347 Pa. 247, ___, 32 A. 2d 27, 29 (1943). Thus, the implied boundaries of the common area may be inferred from the design of the building. As the Court said in *Parsons,* where "the possessor gives the other person reason to believe that his presence is permitted or desired," the landlord might be liable. *Id.* ___, 32 A. 2d 30.

Under the implicit test, the plywood door is a common door because it abutted a common foyer and appeared to lead to other areas of the building. Moreover, not only was the door open, but Wharton also had invited party-goers to "look around," implying that open doors could be used for passage. Revere may analogize that a similar open door in *Portee* was considered a common doorway. But Wharton may distinguish *Portee* because the doorway led from a common hallway to a common basement area. The plywood door, however, did not lead to a common area beyond the first few steps.

(3) The renovation area was not common under either the express or implicit test.

In contrast to the foyer, the commercial renovation area was not expressly intended for common use. The area was normally securely locked, and it had not been jointly used by several tenants.

In contrast to the door, and even under the implicit test, the renovation area is likely not a common area. Only if Wharton gave Revere "reason to believe that his presence was permitted" would the renovation area be a common one by implication (*Parsons*). However, even in *Parsons*, a crowd of hotel guests and patrons could not reasonably use a hotel balcony as a waiting room to watch a parade. In support of a jury verdict and the trial court's instructions, the Court in *Parsons* quoted prior precedent and the Restatement, Torts §343 to limit the implied permissible use of the hotel balcony:

> "The mere fact that the possessor knows that . . . a particular visitor is likely, through curiosity or otherwise, to go into parts of the premises where his presence has no relation to the business or affairs of the possessor is not enough to bring such places within the area of business invitation." *Parsons* ____, 32 A. 2d 30.

Wharton will use *Parsons'* scope of invitation analysis as persuasive authority in defining the implied scope of common areas. It is doubtful that the open door and invitation to "look around" would be enough to create a reasonable belief that Revere could use the entire renovation area as a common passageway to search for nearly finished apartments. After the first few steps, the darkened condition and the stud walls should have alerted Revere that he was wandering far beyond any common area. Accordingly, the commercial renovation area was not a common area under the implicit test.

C. *Wharton's established duty of care in common areas includes the duty to inspect, to maintain, repair, and safeguard, and to issue proper warnings concerning common area dangers, and thus there may be no duty in this case for the noncommon renovation area.*

Wharton's broadly stated duty of reasonable care specifically requires her to inspect common areas for unknown dangers, to maintain, repair, and safeguard known defects, and to issue proper warnings concerning discovered dangers. This duty traditionally applies only within the boundaries of the common areas. Therefore, there may be no breach of duty in this case because Wharton's duty would not extend into the noncommon renovation area. Even if Wharton has a duty, a factual question remains whether Wharton had enough time to inspect the first floor foyer and to either close the door or issue proper warnings.

Normally, where a landlord does not know about defective conditions in common areas, she nonetheless has an affirmative duty of reasonable inspection. For example, a landlord has a duty to discover whether a fire escape is dangerous because of rusted I-beams and bolts. *Bowser v. Actman,* 363 Pa. 388, ____, 69 A. 2d 836, 837-838 (1950). Similarly, where a landlord had a month to discover a dangerous door hinge protruding at a basement doorway, he breached his duty of reasonable inspection. *Portee v. Kronzek.* However, Wharton need not inspect the building constantly. The question is whether she had reasonable time to discover the unlocked door and dangerous hole during the evening of the party. This may ultimately be a jury issue, although the presence of numerous party-goers gave her clear reason to inspect.

Once Wharton discovered the danger, she would have had a duty to close the door, repair the hole, or safeguard the danger. (*Bowser*) Alternatively, Wharton might have issued a proper warning about the dangerous hole. *See,* Restatement (Second) of Torts §360 (1965). Even though Wharton did not know about the hole, Revere can reasonably argue that Wharton had a duty to warn visitors that dangerous first floor renovations were under way. All of the Pennsylvania common area cases involve injuries in common areas, *Williams* (common aisle) and *Portee* (common door and stairway), or defects within common areas, *Parsons* (defective balcony) and *Bowser* (defective fire escape). Thus, the Court may conclude that Wharton's duties were coextensive with the common areas. Because Revere was outside the common areas, Wharton had no duty and breached no duty. Despite the case law, Wharton may have had an additional duty to prevent access from a common area to the dangerous renovation site. This issue merits further discussion in the following section.

D. *Revere might still recover if his fall was proximately caused by Wharton's breaching a common area duty to prevent access to dangerous areas.*

Even if Revere were injured in a hole not located in a common area, Wharton may be liable for negligently permitting access from a common area or for negligently failing to warn that dangerous renovations were under way. Only if Revere must have been injured in a common area in order for him to recover would Wharton not be liable under this theory. Unfortunately, Pennsylvania common area law does not directly address the negligent access theory, making prediction uncertain.

Revere will use *Parsons* and *Bowser*, arguing that both involved breaches of inspection and repair duties resulting in injuries on the sidewalks below, areas outside the common areas. Wharton had a duty to inspect the common foyer and a duty to safeguard dangers or issue warnings. Had she closed the plywood door or warned party-goers about the dangerous conditions, Revere's injury could not have happened. Therefore, under *Parsons* and *Bowser*, the breach of Wharton's duties in common areas proximately caused Revere's own access to and subsequent fall into the dangerous hole.

E. *Although summary judgment may be granted on some common area issues, Revere can argue that there are factual disputes.*

Wharton may attempt to obtain summary judgment on four common area issues: (1) that the renovation area was not common, (2) that she had no knowledge of the open door or dangerous hole, (3) that she may not be held liable for negligently permitting access to the noncommon renovation area, and (4) that she breached no duty of care, even of inspection, with respect to the common area. Although there is some support for deciding premises liability issues as a matter of law on undisputed facts, Revere may counterargue that there are reasonable inferences and jury questions on the boundaries of the common areas, Wharton's knowledge of the dangers, and her breach of her duty of care.

In Pennsylvania, motions for summary judgment are governed by 42 P.S. Rule 1035, stating in relevant part that summary judgment may be granted:

> "If the pleadings, depositions, answers to interrogatories, and admissions on file, together with the affidavits, if any, show that there is no genuine issue as to any material fact and that the moving party is entitled to a judgment as a matter of law."

Under Rule 1035, the Court must view the record in the light most favorable to the nonmoving party, giving him the benefit of all favorable inferences. *Kent* v. *Miller*, 222 Pa. Super. 390, 294 A. 2d 821 (1972). The burden of proving the absence of disputed facts rests on the moving party, in this case Wharton. *Michigan Bank* v. *Steenson*, 211 Pa. Super. 405, 236 A. 2d 565 (1967).

No Pennsylvania cases directly address the appropriateness of summary judgment in resolving issues of common area liability. Before the adoption of the rules of civil procedure, the Court determined issues of premises liability as a matter of law. *Borman* v. *United Merchant's Realty and Improvement Company*, 264 Pa. 158, 107 A. 682 (1919). In *Borman*, the defendant's objection was sustained when the pleaded facts showed that plaintiff was injured by walking through a first story door while looking for an entrance to the second floor. Instead, plaintiff fell down the basement stairs. The Court reasoned that a jury would be unable to conclude that there was anything about the door that could indicate a finding of negligence because no reasonable person could have been so misled. *Id.* 160, 107 A. 684.

Revere can argue that there are several material law-fact disputes. Juries have frequently determined the exact boundaries of disputed common areas. *Portee* v. *Kronzek* (basement stairway); *Bowser* v. *Artman* (hotel balcony). Whether Wharton breached her duty of care is also a classic jury issue. Finally, Wharton's subjective knowledge of the dangerous conditions, including the open door and the unguarded hole, are also factual issues. Revere can argue that Wharton should not get summary judgment on a question of subjective knowledge based on her own self-serving statements, especially when she had an undisputed opportunity to observe the dangers.

Brief

Argument:
A jury may find defendant landlord liable to Revere for failing to safeguard the common areas of One Traverso Street.

A. *Defendant landlord has a statutory and common law duty to Revere with respect to the common areas of One Traverso Street.*

As the owner and landlord of One Traverso Street, a multiple dwelling premise with three or more residential units, defendant Wharton has a statutory "duty of reasonable care for safety in use" of the "common facilities" of the building over which she "retains control." 68 Pa. Cons. Stat. Ann. §250.551 (3) and 250, 552 (Purdon). Defendant's common area duty protects Revere whether he is viewed as a social guest of tenant Paul Cohen or as a prospective tenant for an available apartment. *Id.* Not only is Revere protected by the act, he also has a common law cause of action against defendant landlord for any breach of her duty to safeguard common areas. *Portee v. Kronzek,* 194 Pa. Sup. 193, ____, 166 A. 2d 328, 331 (1960). Count II seeks recovery both under the act and at common law.

B. *Summary judgment is inappropriate because several key issues must go to the jury.*

Summary judgment on Count II should be denied both because several law-fact issues in this case have historically been left for the jury and because certain material facts are in substantial dispute. As argued below, juries have consistently determined the exact boundaries of disputed common areas. Whether defendant breached her legal duties is also a classic jury issue. Defendant's subjective knowledge of the dangerous conditions in and near the undisputed common areas is another factual issue. Finally, defendant's duty to prevent foreseeable access to dangerous areas is essentially a factual controversy. Pursuant to 42 P.S. Rule 1035, this Court must take the view of the record most favorable to the plaintiff, giving him the benefit of all favorable inferences. The burden of proving the absence of any factual dispute rests on defendant Wharton, a burden she cannot possibly carry. *Michigan Bank v. Steenson,* 211 Pa. Sup. 405, 236 A. 2d 565 (1967).

C. *A jury could find that defendant landlord gave Revere reason to believe that the open foyer doorway and the area beyond were intended for his common use.*

By her design of the entrance foyer, by the open door leading off of the common foyer, and by her open-ended oral invitation, defendant landlord extended an implied invitation to William Revere, permitting him to inspect the accessible areas of the building's first floor. Because a jury could reasonably conclude that Wharton gave Revere reason to believe he could make common use of the open doorway and area beyond, the boundaries of the common areas of One Traverso Street are in dispute. Accordingly, summary judgment is inappropriate.

Defendant Wharton is liable for the dangerous conditions in the common "passageways" of One Traverso Street over which she "retains control." 68 Pa. Cons. Stat. Ann. §250.552 (Purdon). Not only is Wharton responsible for expressly retained common areas such as the first floor foyer, she is also legally responsible for the dangerous conditions existing in areas she implicitly held open for common use of tenants and their guests.

Parsons v. *Drake*, 347 Pa. 247, _____, 32 A. 2d 27, 30 (1943); *Bowser* v. *Artman*, 363 Pa. 388, _____, 69 A. 2d 836, 838 (1949); cf. *Argo* v. *Goodstein*, 438 Pa. 408, _____, 265 A. 2d 783, 786 (1970).

The essence of the implicit permission test was defined in *Parsons:* "A possessor of land is subject to liability to another . . . for such bodily harm as he sustains upon a part of the land upon which the possessor gives the other *reason to believe* that his presence is permitted or desired." 347 Pa. _____, 32 A. 2d 30, *citing* Restatement of Torts, §343, comment b (emphasis added).

Because the door and area beyond were immediately accessible from the main entrance to the building, Wharton's design of the building itself gave Revere reason to believe that his presence was permitted. As the defendant admits, the doorway and area beyond are presently common passageways, confirming Revere's assessment of the layout. In a similar case, a jury found a basement door off an entrance foyer to be a common passage to a basement speakeasy. *Portee* v. *Kronzek*, 194 Pa. Sup. 193, _____, 166 A. 2d. 328, 329 (1960).

The invitation to use the foyer doorway, implicit in Wharton's design, was reinforced by the door itself being open. In both *Argo* and *Portee*, an open door was pivotal to finding an implied invitation. In *Argo*, a business invitee case, a blind door-to-door salesman fell into an open hole immediately beyond an unlocked door. The Court noted: "Indeed by leaving the door open within easy access of the sidewalk, [the possessor] had issued [the salesman] an implicit invitation." 438 Pa. 265 A. 2d 786. Similarly, in *Portee*, the authorities had removed the basement door during a prior raid on the basement speakeasy. The landlord did not replace the door, and the guest of a speakeasy patron was justified in traversing the open doorway. Like the plaintiffs in *Argo* and *Portee*, Mr. Revere was justified in relying on the open door as an open invitation. Revere's reliance was especially reasonable because Wharton had purposefully left open other doors in the building to facilitate prospective tenants' viewing of available apartments.

Revere did not rely on appearances alone. Defendant landlord voiced an express invitation to Revere and other guests that they "look around" the building without limitation. "Looking around" necessarily means traversing common passageways. It also implies that open areas are open for inspection.

Revere reasonably believed that he was permitted to "look around" and to use the open doorway and area beyond in his search for available apartments. The boundaries of his reasonable belief would define the boundaries of defendant landlord's implied common areas. Defendant landlord attempts to artificially constrict the common areas to the four squares of her own intentions. Whenever the boundaries of common areas are in dispute, juries have always been the final arbiter. *See, e.g., Portee,* 194 Pa. Sup. ____, 166 A. 2d 330; *Bowser,* 363 Pa. ____, 69 A. 2d 838; *cf. Slobodzian v. Beighley,* 401 Pa. 520, ____, 164 A. 2d 923, 924-925 (1960). Therefore, a jury should decide the boundaries of the implied common areas of One Traverso Street.

D. *Defendant landlord could be liable for permitting unsuspecting guests to have easy access to the dangerous renovation area.*

Even if the foyer doorway and the renovation area were not impliedly available for common use, Wharton can still be liable to Revere for permitting his foreseeable access from the undisputed common foyer to the dangerous renovation area. In this case, the open doorway is an actionable defect in the common foyer. There is no stated prerequisite in the act or in the caselaw that common area liability is predicated on injuries actually occurring in a common area.

The Pennsylvania courts have repeatedly applied common negligence principles to common area liability cases. *See e.g., Portee v. Kronzek,* 194 Pa. Sup. 193, 166 A. 2d 328 (1960) (duty of reasonable inspection). In turn, premises liability cases have clearly recognized a negligent access theory.

In a premises liability case involving a business invitee, namely, a blind door-to-door salesman, the Supreme Court held that an occupant could be liable for negligently permitting the salesman's access through an open door to a dangerous hole. *Argo v. Goodstein,* 438 Pa. 408, 265 A. 2d. 783 (1970). Like this case, *Argo* involved a building undergoing renovations. And like the jury may conclude in this case, the Court concluded: "All he had to do was keep the door locked. . . . We uphold the finding of the jury that the appellant was negligent. *He should have locked the door." Id.* ____, 265 A. 2d 787-788 (emphasis added). Two other analogous cases also support plaintiff's negligence access theory. *Slobodzian v. Beighley,* 401 Pa. 520, 163 A. 2d 923 (1960) (access to open cellarway in dark parking lot); *Borman v. United Merchants' Realty & Improvement Co.,* 264 Pa. 136, 107 A. 2d 682 (1919) (plaintiff might have alleged basement door was misleading).

Common area liability is not predicated on an injury occurring in the common area. It is enough that a defect occur in the common area even if it results in injury elsewhere: *e.g., Bowser v. Artman,* 363 Pa. 388, 69 A. 2d 836 (1949) (common fire escape collapsed; injury on pavement below); *cf. Parsons v. Drake,* 347

Pa. 247, 32 A. 2d 27 (1943) (hotel balcony collapsed; injury on pavement below). Because the open door may itself be considered a defect in the common foyer, Revere has satisfied any locus requirement in his common area theory.

E. *A jury could infer that Wharton had actual knowledge of the open door and dangerous hole.*

A major thesis of defendant landlord's motion for summary judgment is that she lacked actual knowledge of the open foyer door and dangerous hole in the renovation area. However, Wharton knew of the extensive damage to the floor, and she knew for several weeks that Rayman planned to remove rotten floorboards in the renovation area near the foyer. A jury might reasonably infer that Wharton thereby had actual knowledge of the hole and chose to disbelieve her self-serving assertion to the contrary. Similarly, Wharton had ample opportunity to observe the open foyer door when she entered the premises. Opportunity to observe is sufficient to permit the jury to infer that Wharton had actual knowledge of the means of access to the dangerous renovation area.

Once Wharton has actual knowledge of the defects, she has a clear duty to safeguard them or to issue proper warnings, both of which she failed to do. *Papa v. Pittsburg Penn-Center Corporation*, 421 Pa. 228, 218 A. 2d 783, 786 (1966) (dictum).

F. *A jury could find that defendant landlord breached her duty to inspect common areas and to issue proper warnings to Revere.*

Even if Wharton did not have actual knowledge of the open door and dangerous hole, a jury could find that she had sufficient time during her three hours at the premises to fulfill her duty to inspect and safeguard the common areas, especially in light of the known renovations and anticipated floor repairs. Similarly, a jury could find that Wharton failed her duty to warn unsuspecting guests such as Revere about the dangerous ongoing renovations on the first floor. Not only did she fail to warn, she actually uttered a misleading open invitation to disaster.

In an analogous case, the Supreme Court has specifically held that three hours is enough time to require a landlord to discover a dangerous condition in a common area. *Papa v. Pittsburg Penn-Center Corporation*, 421 Pa. 227, 218 A. 2d 783 (1966). In *Papa*, water from patrons' shoes and snow from an open window rendered a tiled hallway dangerously slippery. The Court found liability, stating, "Had the landlord performed a reasonable inspection, he would have become aware of this condition." *Id.* ____, 218 A. 2d 786. The same can be said of Wharton.

Wharton also had a duty to issue proper warnings concerning the renovation area. *Argo* v. *Goodstein*, 438 Pa. 408, ____, 265 A. 2d 783, 787-788 (1970). A sign, a light, or a simple word of caution could have warned Revere and prevented his injury. *cf.* *Slobodzian* v. *Beighley*, 401 Pa. 520, 164 A. 2d 923 (1960) (supermarket's failure to light unguarded hole in parking lot was a failure to warn). Wharton's failure to warn is all the more egregious given her knowledge that unsuspecting guests might have access to the known dangerous renovation area. Wharton's egregious failure to warn is further exacerbated by her careless open invitation to "look around" the building. Her open-ended permission and open door were invitations to the disaster that befell Mr. Revere.

Comment

All the differences between memoranda and briefs come into play in the argument section. Whereas the memorandum proceeds in an exploratory fashion, explaining the statute and determining how best to serve the client, the brief asserts an opinion and then persuasively discusses the rationale behind that opinion.

In the memorandum, the writer discusses avenues open to Revere, and finally decides, asserting that the number of material-fact disputes will prevent Wharton from winning summary judgment. Accordingly, the brief begins by discussing the key issues of the case that necessitate a jury trial. The writer loses no opportunity to persuade the reader—he refers to the breach of common area duties as a "classic jury issue," driving home the point emotionally as well as logically.

As in the questions presented and the summary of argument, the argument in the brief proceeds logically, building one section on the foundation of the previous one. The argument establishes Wharton's legal duty, lists the issues that traditionally go to a jury, then discusses the grounds for finding Wharton liable. Note the inclusion of the opponent's view and the subsequent turning of that view to Revere's advantage. In section F, for example, the writer uses the "even if" structure to make his point. *Even if* Wharton didn't know about the dangerous hole (as the opponents would assert), she still had three hours time to inspect the premises and safeguard the area. And even if she didn't have time to inspect, at least she should have had the courtesy to warn the guests about the renovation site. By using the opponents' assertions as springboards to Revere's strong arguments, the writer effectively undercuts the opposition while reinforcing the logic of his own position.

Memorandum

Conclusion:

Revere was not injured in a common area unless he reasonably believed that the renovation area was common and unless his belief is material in defining common area boundaries. Nonetheless, Wharton is potentially liable to Revere under the act and at common law by permitting access to and failing to warn about the dangerous renovations directly accessible from the common foyer. If Wharton can convince the jury that she did not have reasonable time to inspect the foyer and safeguard the hole, or if she can convince the judge that common area liability is predicated solely on dangerous conditions causing injury in common areas, she may avoid liability. Further premise liability research is needed to find persuasive authority on the negligent access theory and the time periods for reasonable inspection.

Brief

Conclusion:

A jury may fairly conclude the open door and area beyond were implicitly held open as common areas for Revere's use. Alternatively, the jury could find that Wharton negligently permitted foreseeable access from the common foyer to the dangerous hole. Not only could the jury find that Wharton had actual knowledge of the hole and open door, it could also find that she had ample opportunity to discover and safeguard the dangerous conditions. Finally, a jury could find that Wharton breached her duty to warn and instead issued an open invitation to disaster. Given the numerous grounds upon which the jury could find in Revere's favor, the Court should deny defendant's motion for summary judgment on Count II.

Respectfully submitted,
By his attorney,

Comment

In both the memorandum and the brief, the conclusions are rel-tively short. By writing such concise prose, the attorney can re-focus the reader's attention on the major points and the logic behind them—but can do so in a form the reader can grasp with a single effort of mind. If the concluding section sprawls on for several paragraphs, it becomes more a part of the analysis or argument than a succinct "wrap-up."

The major difference between the two conclusions is again the admission in the memorandum that there are several possibil-ities open and that Wharton may avoid liability if she can con-vince the jury she had no time to inspect the area. The attorney uses the conclusion to recommend the best route for Revere: proceed with the common area liability theory and do some fur-ther research for persuasive authority on the time needed for inspection. In the brief, the writer reasserts the "numerous grounds" upon which the jury could find in Revere's favor. By this time, the additional research has been done, and the writer asserts with authority that Wharton had ample opportunity to safeguard the dangerous area. The attorney ends with the pow-erful suggestion that Wharton not only breached her duty but "issued an open invitation to disaster."

As this comparison between the memorandum and the trial brief shows, the key to effective legal writing is to know the pur-pose of the document and the specific needs of the audience who will read it. Once the writer establishes those rhetorical ele-ments and really keeps them in mind, legal writing becomes a form *communicating* the law, not an exercise further entangling both the writer and the reader in the web of disconnected legal terms and theories. Writing clear legal prose means not only understanding the law, but also understanding strategies for expressing it.

Appendix:
Case Files
Used as Examples

Vivian Casterbank v. The South End Family Planning Clinic

William Revere v. Jan Wharton, Nelson Rayman, and John Doe

BRIEF FACT STATEMENTS*

Casterbank v. The South End Clinic

Vivian Casterbank, a registered nurse, was employed by the South End Family Planning Clinic, Inc. (clinic), a licensed abortion clinic, on May 26, 1984. On August 10, 1984, Casterbank refused to participate in a minor's abortion because she suspected the parents had not been notified pursuant to the Michigan Parental Notice Act and clinic rules. She also theatened to report the clinic and doctor to state licensing authorities. On August 13, 1984, Casterbank was fired. She claims she was intentionally and tortiously terminated in violation of public policy and that the clinic violated the Whistleblower's Protection Act. She also claims intentional infliction of emotional distress.

As a result of her discharge, Casterbank has been hospitalized and now suffers a psychological disability. She has also suffered humiliation, damage to her professional reputation, loss of wages, loss of earning capacity, and extreme emotional distress.

Revere v. Wharton

On July 22, 1983, Jan Wharton was the landlord of One Traverso Street, which had three or more residential households. William Revere was a social guest at a tenant's party also attended by Wharton. During the evening, Wharton said to the party-goers that three apartments would soon be available, and the guests should "feel free to look around." Revere heard this statement and proceeded to look at those nearly finished apartments with open doors.

Located directly off the main entrance, the first floor foyer is open and used for access to the second and third floors. The normally locked plywood door at the right rear of the foyer was open the night of the party. Through that door lay the renovation area, which, unknown to Wharton, had a dangerous hole. This

---

*Detailed fact patterns are given on the following pages.

unlighted area had stud walls and was clearly undergoing construction. During his "look around," Revere walked through the plywood doorway, passed through a stud wall, and eventually fell into the hole, sustaining serious personal injuries.

CASE ONE (INFORMAL INTERVIEW SUMMARY FORMAT):
Vivian Casterbank v. The South End Family Planning Clinic

Casterbank Applies for Job

On May 1, 1984, an opening existed in the nursing staff as a result of personnel turnover. Advertisements for the opening were posted in area hospitals, and an advertisement was run for a period of two weeks in the local newspapers. The job description was as follows: "A progressive family planning and abortion clinic desires an experienced OB-GYN nurse, R.N., to work a regularly scheduled daytime shift. Duties will include both patient counseling and assist in abortion procedures. Salary beginning at $24,500, previous experience required. Please contact Patricia Jones 288-9822 to discuss this position. This employer is an affirmative action employer."

Vivian Casterbank was an R.N. working swing shifts at General Hospital in the OB-GYN department. Vivian was 38 years old and had received her R.N. nursing certificate in 1967, when she had trained at St. Elizabeth's Hospital, Covington, Kentucky. Vivian had worked OB/GYN for seven years in a hospital in Cincinnati, Ohio, and had thereafter moved to the city of your jurisdiction in 1974 following a job change by her husband. In 1975, Vivian's 8-year-old daughter had died in a motor vehicle accident. Vivian had an extended medical leave from work at the time while suffering from severe depression. Because of the strain of this tragedy and because of other marital problems, Vivian was divorced in 1978. From the time of her move to the city of your jurisdiction, she had worked in the OB-GYN department at General Hospital except for the four-month leave of absence. In her job at the General Hospital, Vivian worked swing shifts, which meant that she worked two weeks consecutively from 7 A.M. to 3:30 P.M., two weeks from 3:30 P.M. until 11:30 P.M., and two weeks consecutively from 11:00 P.M. to 7:00 A.M. She also had to work every third weekend and every third holiday. Although Vivian had adjusted, over time, to the disorientation of working swing shift, she was interested in having a regular shift. Vivian saw the advertisement for the South End Clinic job in the Sunday newspaper. She called Pat Jones and arranged for an interview on May 4, 1984. When she arrived, Vivian first filled out an employment application (which might be available later). She had an interview with Pat Jones during which Ms. Jones, who is the administrator of the Clinic, discussed the salary, working conditions, and the general philosophy of the Clinic. Ms. Jones described the Clinic's commitment to positive employee relations and the fact that they had regularly scheduled conferences to discuss any problems. She also disclosed that a substantial portion of the Clinic's practice involved abortions, including minors' abortions. Ms. Jones asked Vivian if she had any objection to assisting in abortion procedures, and Vivian responded "no," that she had occasionally assisted in such procedures while at the General Hospital. Ms. Jones said that there was a policy manual that would be distributed to her if she were hired that would explain the protocols and procedures at the clinic. At the end of the interview, Ms. Jones expressed a strong interest in Vivian's application, and Vivian stated her willingness to accept the position if it were offered to her. She asked that, if she were hired, she be given two weeks to give notice to her present employer. On May 10, 1984, Patricia Jones called Vivian and offered her the position. She was to start work on May 28, 1984. Vivian accepted, whereupon she received the letter from Pat Jones attached as Exhibit 1.

Casterbank Starts Work

When Vivian reported to work on May 28, 1984, she was given a copy of the procedures and policies handbook and was given a tour of the facility by the head nurse, Rosetta Oliver. Vivian assisted Ms. Oliver that day and the following day as well. On June 4, 1984, she had her first individual assignments. (The procedures and policy manual received by Vivian contained all the sections discussed previously in this memo.) On June 1, 1984, a memo was sent to the employees concerning the now effective date of the Notice/Informed Consent Act.

Vivian's initial regular assignments included intake for both family planning and abortion counseling. Family counseling appointments were scheduled for one-half hour, and abortion counseling sessions were scheduled for forty-five minutes. During her abortion counseling, Vivian would discuss available options, at least a summary of the medical risks involved, and the other issues discussed in the handbook. In the course of her appointments, Vivian would do routine nursing physicals and naturally had responsibility for writing up a medical history of the details of her examination and the issues discussed with the patient on the intake sheet. If the patient expressed further interest in an abortion at the end of the counseling session, Vivian would tell the physician and report on her interview. The patient would then be seen by the physician who would, among other things, obtain written informed consent.

Beginning in mid-July 1984, Vivian was asked for the first time to assist in abortion procedures. She was given additional training by Ms. Oliver and participated in two abortion sessions a week, each three and a half hours long. The first three weeks of abortion session work were uneventful though somewhat stressful for Vivian. She assisted in approximately six to eight abortions per session and regularly worked with Dr. Mayer. For one session she worked with Dr. Judith Kaplan, one of the founders of the Clinic. During the first six sessions, Vivian assisted in approximately forty abortions, twelve of which were minors' abortions.

The policy and procedures manual had an express provision dealing with the issue of parental notice concerning a minor's abortion. This provision was stressed to Vivian in her training, and she was obsessively concerned about compliance given the emphasis in training and the memo describing the criminal provision of the Notice/Informed Consent Act. As previously stated, the manual contained an additional provision that the nurse assisting the physician in the abortion procedure was responsible for checking the medical file, which was to be present in the operating room, to make certain that all necessary documents were on file. As discussed, the Clinic also had a regular procedure, of which Vivian was informed, that provided that a previously scheduled minor's abortion would be posted on the daily schedule only if the parental notice return receipt or telephone verification form had been received by the Clinic. In the twelve minor's abortions in which Vivian had assisted in her earlier sessions, the parental notice receipts had uniformly been present in the files.

J.H. Abortion

On August 10, 1984, Vivian was assigned to assist Dr. Kaplan for the second time. The session was from 1 o'clock to 4:30 in the afternoon. Six abortions were scheduled on the daily schedule, including an abortion at 4 o'clock involving Janet Hill.

The medical file on Janet Hill indicated that she had come to the Clinic for the first time on August 3, 1984. At that time her pregnancy was confirmed; she was diagnosed to be approximately eight and a half weeks pregnant. She was fifteen and a half years old, as verified by her previous treating physician, Dr. Hellman. She had an older brother and a younger sister, was going to be in the eleventh grade, and was living with both parents. The intake sheet (which might be available later) stated that she was going with an older boyfriend her parents did not like and that her family was religious. The file noted that she had been given a sheet explaining the risks of abortion and the alternatives to abortion. The intake sheet stated that she talked about her fear in telling her parents about her pregnancy. She thought they would try to stop her from seeing her boyfriend but not that they would interfere with the abortion. When informed about the parental notice requirement, Ms. Hill seemed relieved and said that might make it easier for her to talk to them, but she would wait till they got the notice.

At the time of her scheduled abortion, Janet Hill was in an agitated state. Vivian had not met with Ms. Hill before because she did not do intake on Ms. Hill's case. Preferred procedure was that the intake nurse would be the assisting nurse, but Vivian was just doing a vacation schedule now. Vivian spent a couple of minutes talking with Ms. Hill and trying to reassure her prior to the arrival of Dr. Kaplan. When Dr. Kaplan arrived, she took Ms. Hill aside to spend a minute or two discussing the procedure with her again. During that interval, Vivian looked through the file pursuant to hospital procedures. In her review of the file, she found the informed consent form, but she could not find the parental notice receipt or telephone verification. She spent thirty seconds or so looking over her desk and behind her desk for the document and couldn't find it. When Dr. Kaplan turned around from her conference with Ms. Hill, Vivian informed the doctor that the parental notice of verification was not in the file. At that point Ms. Hill stated that she had talked with her parents about the abortion on Monday after they got the notice and that both her parents had favored her abortion decision. Vivian asked Ms. Hill if she had seen her parents sign the receipt or if she had seen the notice, and she said no. Vivian said that she did not see the document in the file and that she had noted that Ms. Hill had expressed anxiety about talking to her parents. Vivian asked her again whether she had actually discussed the abortion with her parents and if they had received notice. Vivian told her that the procedure could not be performed without a signed parental notice receipt or telephone verification. At that point Ms. Hill broke down and started crying, and the doctor spent a couple of seconds trying to comfort her. Dr. Kaplan asked Vivian to step to the side, at which time Dr. Kaplan stated that she believed that Ms. Hill had discussed the abortion and that her parents had notice and that Janet was obviously upset about Vivian's accusation. Dr. Kaplan also stated that Ms. Hill was mature for her age and that her pregnancy was only three and a half weeks from the end of the first trimester. Vivian in turn stated that she would not assist in the procedure until and unless the parental notice verification was in the file and that she was doing this pursuant to the clinic handbook. Dr. Kaplan frowned, turned to Ms. Hill, and asked her if there was a number at which her parents could be reached. Ms. Hill responded that her parents had the notice, but she gave the home phone number. Dr. Kaplan called and no one answered. Janet sobbed and asked what was going to happen about her abortion. Dr. Kaplan soothed Janet and then took Vivian's arm and asked her to go out in the hallway with her. She told Ms. Hill that she would be back in a minute. Dr. Kaplan spoke to Vivian in the hall and told her again that she believed the patient and that the parents had been notified. She referred to the fact that the abortion was scheduled on the daily schedule, which confirmed receipt of the return receipt. Vivian stated again that she refused to assist in the abortion because of the handbook and that, if Dr. Kaplan performed the abortion without the necessary parental notice, she would report Dr. Kaplan and the Clinic to the state licensing agencies because she didn't want to lose her license. Dr. Kaplan said, "Don't be absurd," and Vivian said, "You can't make me assist in this abortion." Dr. Kaplan again urged Vivian to assist in the abortion, and Vivian again refused and stated that she would not perform an illegal abortion. Dr. Kaplan, who was red in the face and clearly angry, went to the head nurse and got another nurse to assist in the abortion. At 5 P.M. Vivian's shift ended, and she went home for the weekend.

Casterbank's Discharge

On Monday August 13, 1984, Vivian called in sick because she was upset about Friday. On Tuesday she reported to work at 8:30 A.M. and was immediately summoned to Patricia Jones's office. Ms. Jones asked Vivian to describe to her what had happened on Friday, and Vivian told her in sum and substance what is recited above. Pat Jones asked specifically whether or not she had refused to obey Dr. Kaplan's order, and Vivian stated that she had. She also stated that she felt she was upholding the Clinic's rules in that she could not in good conscience assist in a questionable or illegal abortion. Pat asked Vivian if she had threatened to report Dr. Kaplan and the Clinic to state licensing authorities, and Vivian said yes that she had. Pat Jones asked, "How could you do that when we are in such a hostile political environment?" At that point Pat Jones asked Vivian to return to her normally scheduled nursing duties for that day. Following her lunch break at 1:30 P.M., Vivian was again called in to Pat Jones's office, whereupon Pat Jones told her that she was sorry but that she would have to dismiss her. She stated that she was sorry that Vivian's employment had not worked out but that the Clinic could not function if people had inflexible attitudes and that it couldn't function if employees did not at first try to resolve their complaints internally. Upon Vivian's request Pat Jones had a termination letter written up that reads as follows:

> To Vivian Casterbank: Effective 5 o'clock P.M. on Tuesday, August 14, 1984, your employment with South End Family Planning Clinic, Inc., is terminated. Although the Clinic would be happy to give you a reference in the future, this termination is necessary

given your refusal to assist Dr. Kaplan in a scheduled abortion as instructed and given your threat to bring your grievance to public agencies without first seeking resolution within the Clinic. Very truly yours, Patricia Jones, Director.

Vivian asked if it would be possible for her to go home immediately because she had no further interest in completing her day's work. Patricia said that it was possible and that in any event she would be paid two weeks severance pay despite the short term of her employment.

Vivian went home and couldn't sleep during the night of August 14, 1984. During the following day, she became increasingly depressed and eventually on August 19, 1984, presented herself to the emergency ward at a local hospital for psychiatric counseling. She went to the clinic because she was having suicidal ideation and because she had been unable to eat and virtually unable to sleep. Given the severity of her subjective complaint, she was immediately admitted to the psychiatric wing at the hospital, where she stayed for a one-week admission. Upon her discharge she was assigned to an affiliated psychologist for individual counseling sessions. The week after her discharge from the psychiatric clinic, she contacted a law firm in the city of our jurisdiction. She remains unable to work at this time. (Medical records will be available later for associates.)

At the time of Vivian's discharge, Pat Jones had not been able to locate the parental notice receipt, although she had spoken to the employee responsible for receiving the receipts and composing the daily abortion schedules. In a thorough search of the Clinic, the receipt has never been located. However, after contacting Casterbank's lawyer, the Clinic by its attorneys contacted Mr. and Mrs. Hill, who will confirm by affidavit that they received notice prior to August 10, 1984.

Casterbank's Injuries

In addition to her one-week hospitalization, Casterbank continues to suffer from what has been diagnosed as an obsessive compulsive neurosis, schizophrenia with a well-developed obsessional component, and reactive depression secondary to job loss. Given the severity of her decompensation and the reemergence of deep-seated conflicts, Vivian's treating physicians are pessimistic about her prospects for a quick recovery.

Vivian's treating physicians are of the opinion that her discharge from the clinic was a substantial contributing factor to her breakdown and her disability. It is estimated that Vivian will be totally disabled for two or more years and partially disabled for an additional two years.

During her period of total disability, Vivian will need individual counseling two times a week; during partial disability, she will need one session a week. Thereafter, Vivian will need monthly counseling and continuation of her medication.

Vivian is concerned about her wage loss, her medical expenses, damage to her professional reputation, and the humiliation, embarrassment, and severe mental distress she feels because of this "unfair" discharge. Naturally, she is also concerned about her disability.

Clinic's Concern About Publicity

Since contacted by Casterbank's attorney, the Clinic is very concerned about publicity. It is in the process of seeking alternative sources of funding, and "right to life" groups have been picketing another abortion clinic, which threatens its survival. The Clinic is desperate to avoid publicity.

CASE TWO (FORMAL COMPLAINT FORMAT):
William Revere v. Jan Wharton, Nelson Rayman, and John Doe

STATE OF _____

COUNTY, §.

SUPERIOR
COURT
CIVIL ACTION
NO. 98765

WILLIAM REVERE,	)	
Plaintiff,	)	
VS.	)	COMPLAINT
JAN WHARTON,	)	
NELSON RAYMAN, and	)	
JOHN DOE,	)	
Defendants.	)	

1   This is an action for money damages for injuries suffered by the plaintiff as a result of a dangerous condition on the premises of the Defendant Wharton. This dangerous condition was negligently caused by the Defendant Wharton and/or her agents, Defendant Nelson Rayman and Defendant John Doe.

PARTIES

2   The Plaintiff, William Revere, is a resident of City, County, State.

3   The Defendant Jan Wharton is a resident of City, County, State. Jan Wharton is, and at all times relevant to this action was, the owner of and in control of the building numbered One Traverso Street, City, County, State (hereinafter "the premises").

4   The Plaintiff is informed and believes, and therefore states, that the Defendant Nelson Rayman is a resident of City, County, State. At all times relevant to this action, the Defendant Nelson Rayman was, by virtue of a contract with the Defendant Wharton, actively involved in converting the premises from a warehouse to residential and commercial space for rental.

5   At all times relevant to this action, the Defendant "John Doe" was an employee, servant, or agent of the Defendant Wharton and/or the Defendant Rayman and was actively involved in converting the premises from a warehouse to residential and commercial space for rental. The true name and capacity of the Defendant herein referred to as John Doe by this fictitious name. Plaintiff will seek leave to amend this complaint to state the true name and capacity of John Doe when his or her name and capacity have been ascertained.

STATEMENT OF FACTS

6   On or about September 15, 1982, the Defendant Wharton hired the Defendant Rayman to renovate the premises according

to the Defendant Wharton's specifications. The purpose of this renovation was to convert the premises from a warehouse to space for lease to residential and commercial tenants. Said renovation is inherently dangerous.

7   In the course of this renovation, the Defendant Rayman removed or instructed workers to remove, sections of the floorboards from the first floor of the premises.

8   As a result of the removal of these floorboards, a dangerous hole, some 18 feet by 16 feet and 12 feet in depth, was created.

9   No guardrails, toe boards, or protective barriers of any type were placed around this opening. No temporary flooring was installed, nor were there any warnings.

10   Some time after September 1982, but prior to the completion of the renovation of the premises, Defendant Wharton leased to one Paul Cohen a completed residential unit on the second floor of the premises.

11   On or about July 22, 1983, the Plaintiff attended a party given by Paul Cohen and held at Cohen's second floor apartment at the premises. This party was planned by Cohen and the Defendant Wharton wholly or partly for the purpose of showing newly renovated residential units to prospective tenants.

12   At the time of this party, the Plaintiff was actively engaged in a search for a new apartment. He attended the party in order to view an apartment at the premises and to inquire about the possibility of renting an apartment.

13   During the evening, the Defendant Wharton, on several occasions, urged the persons attending the party to view the other apartments in the building. Wharton informed these persons that the doors to the other apartments were unlocked and that they were welcome to inspect the premises.

14   Pursuant to the Defendant Wharton's invitation, the Plaintiff inspected two open apartments on the second floor. He then proceeded to the first floor.

15   On the first floor, the door to the area of the premises then undergoing renovation had been negligently left unlocked and ajar by the Defendant John Doe.

16   Plaintiff entered this area believing he could view an additional apartment.

17   Plaintiff fell into the dangerous hole described in Paragraph 8 above.

18   As a result of this fall, Plaintiff has suffered severe, painful, and permanent injuries to his left leg and hip and has permanently

lost function in that leg and hip. To date, treatment of the Plaintiff's injuries has required ten days hospitalization, surgery, and the placement of pins in his leg.

19   The Plaintiff continues to undergo treatment for his injuries, and he will require future medical treatment, including, without limitation, physiotherapy to aid in the recovery of partial use of his right leg.

20   The Plaintiff's injuries have prevented him from working and have resulted in a loss of wages, pain and suffering, and other damages.

COUNT I: DEFENDANT WHARTON'S NEGLIGENCE

21   Plaintiff here repeats and realleges the allegations of Paragraphs 3 and Paragraphs 6 through 20 of this Complaint the same as if said Paragraphs were expressly restated here.

22   On or about July 22, 1983, while Plaintiff was lawfully on the premises, Plaintiff was caused to fall into the hole described in Paragraph 8 above. Plaintiff's fall was a direct and proximate result of the negligence of Defendant Wharton and/or her employee(s), servant(s), or agent(s).

23   Defendant Wharton negligently permitted a hole in the floor of the premises to remain unguarded.

24   This hole was in an area accessible to persons lawfully on the premises.

25   By virtue of this conduct, the Defendant Wharton failed to keep premises intended for use by invitees such as the Plaintiff in a reasonably safe condition.

26   Defendant Wharton failed to warn lawful visitors of a dangerous condition on the premises.

27   Defendant Wharton failed to lock or otherwise secure the entrance to the construction area on the first floor.

28   As a direct and proximate result of Defendant Wharton's negligence, Plaintiff suffered severe, painful, and permanent injuries to his left leg and hip and other injuries as alleged in Paragraphs 18 through 20 above.

COUNT II: DEFENDANT WHARTON'S LIABILITY FOR A COMMON AREA

29   Plaintiff here repeats and realleges the allegations of Paragraphs 3 and Paragraphs 6 through 20 of this Complaint, the same as if said Paragraphs were expressly restated here.

30   Defendant Wharton rented the premises for residential use to her tenants, including Paul Cohen.

31   By statute and common law, Defendant Wharton is liable for the safety, maintenance, and care of all common areas of the premises, including the first floor foyer and all the doors in the foyer. Wharton's duty of care extends to the tenants and their lawful guests, including Plaintiff Revere.

32   Defendant Wharton breached her duty of care with respect to a common area, the first floor foyer and the doors in the foyer, by failing to inspect the foyer, by permitting the door to remain open, by failing to warn tenants and their guests of the hazardous renovations being performed and of the dangerous hole in the first floor. Defendant Wharton's duties in common areas were nondelegable.

33   As a direct and proximate result of the breach by Defendant Wharton of her duty for common areas, Plaintiff suffered severe, painful, and permanent injuries to his left leg and hip and other injuries, as alleged in Paragraphs 18 through 20 above.

COUNT III: DEFENDANT RAYMAN'S NEGLIGENCE

34   Plaintiff here repeats and realleges the allegations of Paragraphs 4 and Paragraphs 6 through 20 of this Complaint, the same as if said Paragraphs were expressly restated here.

35   On or about July 22, 1983, while Plaintiff was lawfully on the premises, Plaintiff was caused to fall into the hole described in Paragraph 8 above. Plaintiff's fall was a direct and proximate result of the negligence of Defendant Rayman and/or his employee(s), servant(s), or agent(s).

36   Defendant Rayman was negligent in failing to place, or in failing to ensure that his agent(s), servant(s), and/or employee(s) placed protective barriers around or temporary flooring on the hole described in Paragraph 8 above.

37   Defendant Rayman was negligent in failing to lock, or in failing to ensure that his agent(s), servant(s), and/or employee(s) locked the door to the area where the hole was located.

38   As a direct and proximate result of the negligence of the Defendant Rayman and or his agent(s), servant(s), and/or employee(s), Plaintiff suffered severe, painful, and permanent injuries to his left leg and hip and other injuries as alleged in Paragraphs 18 through 20 above.

COUNT IV: NEGLIGENCE OF JOHN DOE

39   Plaintiff here repeats and realleges the allegations of Paragraphs 5 through 20 of this Complaint the same as if said Paragraphs were expressly restated here.

40   On or about July 22, 1983, while Plaintiff was lawfully on the premises, Plaintiff was caused to fall into the hole described in Paragraph 8 above. Plaintiff's fall was a direct and proximate result of the negligence of Defendant John Doe.

41   Defendant Doe was negligent in failing to lock the door to the area in which the hole was located.

42   As a direct and proximate result of Defendant Doe's negligence, Plaintiff suffered severe, painful, and permanent injuries to his left leg and hip and other injuries, as alleged in Paragraphs 18 through 20 above.

COUNT V: DEFENDANT WHARTON'S VICARIOUS LIABILITY FOR THE NEGLIGENCE OF HER AGENTS

43   Plaintiff here repeats and realleges the allegations of Paragraphs 3 through 20 of this Complaint, the same as if said Paragraphs were expressly restated here.

44   On or about July 22, 1983, while Plaintiff was lawfully on the premises, Plaintiff was caused to fall into the opening described in Paragraph 8 above. Plaintiff's fall was a direct and proximate result of the negligence of Defendant Rayman and/or of Defendant John Doe. The opening was inherently dangerous.

45   At the time of Plaintiff's fall, and at all times material to the facts stated herein, Defendant Nelson Rayman and Defendant John Doe were employees of Defendant Jan Wharton and were performing her nondelegable duties.

46   As a result of this employment relationship, Defendant Wharton is vicariously liable for such negligence of the Defendant Rayman and/or the Defendant John Doe.

47   As a direct and proximate result of the negligence of the Defendant Rayman and/or the Defendant John Doe, Plaintiff suffered severe, painful, and permanent injuries to his left leg and hip and other injuries, as alleged in Paragraphs 18 through 20 above.

PRAYER FOR RELIEF

48   WHEREFORE the Plaintiff prays that this Court hold the Defendants individually, jointly, or severally liable and enter judg-

ment against the Defendants, or any of them, in the amount of $1,000,000, plus interest from the date of the commencement of this action, costs, a reasonable attorney's fee, and such other and further relief as this Court may deem just and proper.

Plaintiff demands a trial by jury.

WILLIAM REVERE
By His Attorney

Brook K. Baker
94 Washington Street
City, State
542-4365

Dated: December 8, 1983